# FINCH BAKERY

## DISCO BAKES & PARTY CAKES

# FINCH BAKERY

## DISCO BAKES & PARTY CAKES

### LAUREN & RACHEL FINCH

# CONTENTS

# TIME TO PARTY!

Welcome to our second book – *Finch Bakery: Disco Bakes & Party Cakes* – filled with brand-new recipes perfect for any celebration! From birthday parties to BBQs, Halloween to Christmas, Valentine's Day to Easter, we have compiled some of our favourite recipes for your special occasion.

For those that don't know, we are Lauren and Rachel, twins from Lancashire, UK. Our baking journey began ten years ago when Lauren made our 21st birthday cake. Made from stamped fondant flowers, it caused quite a stir on social media and three years later we opened the doors to our first cake shop. Over the past 7 years, Finch Bakery has grown to nearly 40 staff members, an online shop, a range of baking equipment, a wholesale service, three units, two shops, a van and, of course, we are published authors!

Since our first book, *Finch Bakery*, was released in August 2021, we have opened a brand-new shop and continued to work hard to keep up with the demand. We still use every recipe written in the book to make our freshly baked cookies, blondies, brownies and more, to stock our shops daily. In the first book, we covered most of our top sellers and favourite basic recipes, using easily interchangeable flavours and encouraging people to experiment at home. In this book, we have explored some slightly trickier bakes that wouldn't look out of place on a restaurant menu. Think glossy meringues, fruity crumbles and crème brûlées – all with a Finch Bakery twist! Here you'll find plenty of showstopping celebration cakes for birthdays, wedding days, garden parties and game nights. Plus more of our original bakes such as rocky roads, cookies, cakes and cookie pies for dessert tables, dinner parties, wedding buffets and more. We will guide you through them all with ease, whether you're a novice baker or a professional.

We hope you love this second installment of our new favourite recipes, to enjoy creating at home and celebrating in style.

Lauren & Rachel x

# DEEP PAN COOKIES, COOKIE PIES & COOKIE BARS

# CHERRY BAKEWELL COOKIE PIE

This aesthetically pleasing cookie pie is stuffed to the brim with all things cherry Bakewell. Layered with white chocolate, glacé cherries, blondie and whole cherry Bakewells, this recipe is simple but very effective and interchangeable with different flavour fillings. If almonds are your thing, this pie is for you!

## INGREDIENTS

*Serves 8 or 12*

**Cookie dough**

150g (¾ cup packed) light soft brown sugar

150g (⅔ cup) caster sugar

190g (1 stick plus 4 tbsp) unsalted butter

1 egg plus 1 egg yolk

5–10 drops of almond extract

40g (2 tbsp) golden syrup

285g (2 cups plus 2 tbsp) plain flour

1 tsp baking powder

300g (10oz) white chocolate chips

150g (5½oz) glacé cherries

**Filling**

6 store-bought Cherry Bakewells

3 Cherry Bakewell Blondies (see page 112)

450g (1lb) white chocolate spread (or 450g/1lb white chocolate with 15ml/1 tbsp vegetable oil)

A handful of glacé cherries

**Decoration (optional)**

100g (6½ tbsp) unsalted butter

200g (1⅔ cups) icing sugar

5 drops of almond extract

Pink gel food colouring (optional)

8–12 glacé cherries

## SPECIAL EQUIPMENT

Mixer or hand-held electric whisk

20cm (8in) round cake tin, lined

Piping bag and any open star nozzle

*1* Freeze the cherry Bakewells and blondies to hold their shape.

*2* To make the cookie dough, using a mixer or hand-held electric whisk, cream both sugars and the butter together and add the egg and egg yolk. Mix in the almond extract, golden syrup, flour, baking powder and chocolate chips. If the dough looks sticky, add an extra 10g (3½ tsp) of flour and mix until combined. Hand mix or knead the glacé cherries into the dough.

*3* Taking a spoon or an ice-cream scoop (or your hands), press some of the cookie dough evenly into the bottom of the lined tin. Press more mixture into the sides and leave a gap about 1cm (½in) from the top. Cover and set aside the remaining dough.

*4* Melt the white chocolate spread (or white chocolate mixed with oil). Arrange 5 frozen cherry Bakewells in a circle around the edge of the tin and a sixth in the centre. Roll some of the remaining cookie dough into balls and place in the gaps, alternating with the glacé cherries. Pour over 300g (10oz) of the white chocolate spread, ensuring it gets in all the gaps. Add chunks of cherry Bakewell blondie and fill in more gaps with balls of cookie dough and glacé cherries before pouring over the remaining 150g (5½oz) white chocolate spread, spreading it over with a spoon. Put the tin in the freezer.

*5* Preheat the oven to 195°C (175°C fan/385°F/Gas 5½). After at least 30 minutes in the freezer, use the remaining cookie dough to make a lid for the top of the pie, connecting the edges until completely sealed. Bake for 30 minutes, then leave to cool completely in the tin. Chill in the fridge for at least 6 hours (preferably overnight).

*6* To make the buttercream, if using, combine the butter with the icing sugar and almond extract in a mixer. Use a spatula to marble in some pink food colouring. Transfer to a piping bag fitted with an open star nozzle.

*7* Slice the cookie pie into 8 or 12 pieces and pipe buttercream drop stars onto the top of each piece. Finish with a cherry.

# MINT CHOCOLATE COOKIE PIE

Cookie pies are still all the rage and can be filled with pretty much anything! This cookie pie is stuffed to the brim with all your favourite mint chocolates.

## *INGREDIENTS*

*Serves 8 or 12*

**Cookie dough**

150g (¾ cup packed) light soft brown sugar

150g (⅔ cup) caster sugar

190g (1 stick plus 4 tbsp) unsalted butter

1 egg plus 1 egg yolk

40g (2 tbsp) golden syrup

150g (5oz) milk chocolate chips, plus extra for topping

5–10 drops of peppermint extract

280g (2 cups plus 2 tbsp) plain flour

1 tsp baking powder

20g (¼ cup) cocoa powder

**Filling**

10 After Eight Mint Chocolate Thins

1 large packet Aero Peppermint Bubbles

1 bar Aero mint chocolate

500g (1lb 2oz) white chocolate spread (or 500g/1lb 2oz white chocolate mixed with 40ml/ 2½ tbsp vegetable oil)

Green oil-based food colouring

**Decoration (optional)**

100g (6½ tbsp) unsalted butter

180g (1⅓ cups) icing sugar

Green gel food colouring (optional)

3–5 drops of peppermint extract

## *SPECIAL EQUIPMENT*

Mixer or hand-held electric whisk

20cm (8in) round cake tin, lined

Piping bag and large piping nozzle

*1* Freeze all the mint chocolate bars. This can be done well in advance or a couple of hours before baking.

*2* To make the cookie dough, using a mixer or hand-held electric whisk, cream both sugars and the butter together. Add the egg and egg yolk. Add the golden syrup, chocolate chips and mint extract and sift in the flour, baking powder and cocoa powder. Mix until combined.

*3* Press some of the cookie dough evenly into the lined tin. Press more mixture around the sides of the tin and leave a gap about 2.5cm (1in) from the top. Set aside the remaining cookie dough.

*4* Melt the white chocolate spread (or white chocolate mixed with oil) in a bowl in the microwave and add some green food colouring. Leave to cool slightly.

*5* Cover the bottom of the tin with a mixture of the frozen mint chocolates and balls of cookie dough. Pour over the green chocolate until covered, then repeat, filling the space with more mint chocolates and cookie dough balls (leaving enough cookie dough to make a pie lid).

*6* Put the tin in the freezer and preheat the oven to 195°C (175°C fan/385°F/Gas 5½).

*7* After at least 30 minutes in the freezer, use the remaining cookie dough to make a pie lid, connecting the edges until completely sealed. Push some extra milk chocolate chips into the top. Bake for 30 minutes, then leave to cool completely in the tin. Chill in the fridge for at least 6 hours (preferably overnight).

*8* Remove the cookie pie from the tin and slice into 8 or 12 pieces. To make the mint buttercream, if using, combine the butter with the icing sugar, then add green colouring and 3 drops of mint extract or to taste.

*9* Load a piping bag with a large piping nozzle and pipe whips onto the top of the cookie pie. Decorate with more mint chocolates, if you like.

# RAINBOW COOKIE PIE

Perfect for any birthday party, this cookie pie has bright layers of rainbow chocolate inside our original chewy cookie recipe, topped with M&Ms and sprinkles.

## INGREDIENTS

*Serve 8 or 12*

**Cookie dough**

190g (1 stick plus 4 tbsp) unsalted butter

150g (¾ cup packed) light soft brown sugar

150g (⅔ cup) caster sugar

1 egg plus 1 egg yolk

300g (2½ cups) plain flour

1 tsp baking powder

40g (2 tbsp) golden syrup

60g (2¼oz) bake-stable sprinkles, plus extra for topping

60g (2¼oz) M&Ms, plus extra for topping

150g (5½oz) white chocolate chips

**Filling**

1kg (2lb 4oz) white chocolate spread (or 1kg/2lb 4oz white chocolate mixed with 80ml/ 5½ tbsp vegetable oil)

Pink, orange, yellow, green, blue, indigo and violet oil-based food colourings

**Decoration (optional)**

100g (6½ tbsp) unsalted butter

180g (1⅓ cups) icing sugar

3–5 drops of vanilla extract

## SPECIAL EQUIPMENT

Mixer or hand-held electric whisk

20cm (8in) round cake tin, lined

Piping bag and open star nozzle

1 To make the cookie dough, put the butter and both sugars into a mixer and, using the paddle attachment, cream together on a high speed (or use a hand-held electric whisk). Add the egg and yolk and mix.

2 Sift in the flour and baking powder, then add the remaining cookie dough ingredients. Combine slowly until a dough forms and the sprinkles, M&Ms and chocolate chips are evenly distributed.

3 Press a thick layer of dough evenly into the bottom of the lined tin. Press more mixture around the sides of the tin and leave a gap about 2.5cm (1in) from the top. Cover and set aside the remaining cookie dough.

4 Melt the white chocolate spread (or white chocolate mixed with oil) in a bowl in the microwave and divide between seven bowls. Use the oil-based food colourings to colour each bowl a colour of the rainbow. Carefully pour the last rainbow colour (violet) into the cookie base and set in the freezer until tacky (about 10 minutes). Repeat with each colour, finishing with pink. Return to the freezer.

5 Preheat the oven to 195°C (175°C fan/385°F/Gas 5½).

6 After at least 30 minutes in the freezer, remove the tin and use the remaining cookie dough to make a lid, place it on top and seal the edges. Push some extra M&Ms into the top along with a handful of sprinkles. Bake for 30 minutes. Leave to cool completely in the tin, then chill in the fridge overnight.

7 Slice the pie evenly into 8 or 12 pieces. If decorating with buttercream, whip the butter on a high speed until whitened. Sift in the icing sugar, add the vanilla extract and mix until combined. Load a piping bag with an open star nozzle and pipe whips on top of each slice. Finish with more sprinkles and M&Ms.

# DEEP PAN COOKIES

Think deep pan pizza but they're chewy, chocolatey, delicious cookies instead. Baked inside a 10cm (4in) crumpet ring, this versatile recipe provides perfectly round, deep pan cookies with unlimited flavour combinations. Bake things inside, on top, serve cold, with ice cream or just eat warm straight off the tray. Your guests will be obsessed!

## INGREDIENTS

*Makes 10*

225g (2 sticks) unsalted butter

170g (¾ cup plus 2 tbsp packed) light soft brown sugar

210g (generous 1 cup) caster sugar

10–15 drops of vanilla extract, or to taste (optional)

2 eggs

50g (2½ tbsp) golden syrup

475g (3⅓ cups) plain flour

1 heaped tsp baking powder

150g (5½oz) white chocolate chips, plus extra for topping

150g (5½oz) milk chocolate chips, plus extra for topping

## SPECIAL EQUIPMENT

Mixer

10 x 10cm (4in) cookie/crumpet rings

2 baking trays, lined

Cake release spray or homemade cake release (see page 202) (optional)

1   Preheat the oven to 195°C (175°C fan/385°F/Gas 5½).

2   Put the butter, both sugars and the vanilla extract, if using, into a mixer and, using the paddle attachment, cream together on a high-speed setting (or use a hand-held electric whisk). Add the eggs and golden syrup and mix on a low-speed setting. Sift in the flour and baking powder. Mix together until combined.

3   Add the chocolate chips and mix again. If the dough is too sticky, you may need to add up to an extra 50g (⅓ cup) of flour.

4   Set out five cookie/crumpet rings on each lined baking tray. If using cake release spray or cake release, use on the inside of the rings.

5   Use an ice-cream scoop to pick up mixture and weigh out portions about 140–145g (5oz). Roll each one into a ball and place in the middle of a ring. Flatten slightly with your hand.

6   Add extra chocolate chips to the tops and bake for 14 minutes, or until the tops of the cookies are golden brown. Remove from the oven and drop or bang the baking trays on a hard surface.

7   Leave the cookies to cool in the rings, on the trays. When completely cooled, push out of the rings.

8   Serve straight away on their own, or add toppings, ice cream and more! Or store in an airtight container until ready to eat for up to a week.

**TOP TIPS** ★ We use golden syrup in our cookies for that extra sweetness and a chewier soft texture – but feel free to leave this out.

★ You may need to add up to 100g (¾ cup) of flour depending how sticky the mixture is. This variation could be due to anything from how melted the butter is, to the size of eggs used. If your mixture feels too wet, add a spoonful of flour at a time until the dough comes together. The stickier the mixture, the chewier the cookie will be (which you may like!).

# JAMMIE DODGER
# DEEP PAN COOKIES

## INGREDIENTS

*Makes 10*

225g (2 sticks) unsalted butter

170g (¾ cup plus 2 tbsp packed) light soft brown sugar

210g (generous 1 cup) caster sugar

10–15 drops of vanilla extract, or to taste (optional)

2 eggs

50g (2½ tbsp) golden syrup

475g (3⅓ cups) plain flour

1 heaped tsp baking powder

300g (10oz) white chocolate chips, plus extra for topping

10–15 tsp raspberry or strawberry jam

10 mini Jammie Dodgers

## SPECIAL EQUIPMENT

Mixer

10 x 10cm (4in) cookie/crumpet rings

2 baking trays, lined

Cake release spray or homemade cake release (see page 202) (optional)

Piping bag, with end cut off

*1* Preheat the oven to 195°C (175°C fan/385°F/Gas 5½).

*2* Put the butter, both sugars and the vanilla extract, if using, into a mixer and, using the paddle attachment, cream together on a high-speed setting (or use a hand-held electric whisk). Add the eggs and golden syrup and mix on a low-speed setting. Sift in the flour and baking powder. Mix together until combined.

*3* Add the chocolate chips and mix again. If the dough is too sticky, you may need to add up to an extra 50g (⅓ cup) of flour.

*4* Set out five cookie/crumpet rings on each lined baking tray. If using cake release spray or cake release, use on the inside of the rings.

*5* Use an ice-cream scoop to pick up mixture and weigh out portions about 140–145g (5oz). Roll each one into a ball and place in the middle of a ring. Flatten slightly with your hand, then use the back of a teaspoon (or a thumb) to make a dent in the top of the cookies.

*6* Fill the dents with jam either using a piping bag or a teaspoon. Add a mini Jammie Dodger to the top of each cookie.

*7* Add extra chocolate chips to the tops and bake for 14 minutes, or until the tops of the cookies are golden brown. Remove from the oven and drop or bang the baking trays on a hard surface.

*8* Leave the cookies to cool in the rings, on the trays. When they have partially cooled, push out of the rings and leave to cool completely. Serve or store in an airtight container for up to a week.

# CHERRY BAKEWELL DEEP PAN COOKIES

## INGREDIENTS

*Makes 10*

225g (2 sticks) unsalted butter

170g (¾ cup plus 2 tbsp packed) light soft brown sugar

210g (generous 1 cup) caster sugar

Almond extract, to taste

2 eggs

50g (2½ tbsp) golden syrup

500–550g (3½–scant 4 cups) plain flour

1 heaped tsp baking powder

300g (10oz) white chocolate chips, plus extra for topping

150g (5½oz) glacé cherries, some whole and some halved

### Decoration

50g (⅓ cup) icing sugar

30g (1oz) flaked almonds, toasted (optional)

10 glacé cherries (optional)

## SPECIAL EQUIPMENT

Mixer

10 x 10cm (4in) cookie/crumpet rings

2 baking trays, lined

Cake release spray or homemade cake release (see page 202) (optional)

*1*  Preheat the oven to 195°C (175°C fan/385°F/Gas 5½).

*2*  Put the butter, both sugars and the almond extract into a mixer and, using the paddle attachment, cream together on a high speed (or use a hand-held electric whisk). We usually use about 15–20 drops of almond extract, but it is completely up to your personal preference. Add the eggs and golden syrup and mix on a low-speed setting. Sift in the flour and baking powder. Mix together until combined.

*3*  Add the white chocolate chips and glacé cherries and mix again. If the dough is too sticky, you may need to add up to an extra 50g (⅓ cup) of flour.

*4*  Set out five cookie/crumpet rings on each lined baking tray. If using cake release spray or cake release, use on the inside of the rings.

*5*  Use an ice-cream scoop to pick up mixture and weigh out portions about 140–145g (5oz). Roll each one into a ball and place in the middle of a ring. Flatten slightly with your hand.

*6*  Add extra white chocolate chips to the tops and bake for 14 minutes, or until the tops of the cookies are golden brown. Remove from the oven and drop or bang the baking trays on a hard surface.

*7*  Leave the cookies to cool in the rings, on the trays. When they have partially cooled, push out of the rings and leave to cool completely.

*8*  Mix the icing sugar with a little water to make a water icing and drizzle over the tops of the cookies. Top with some toasted flaked almonds and a glacé cherry, if you like. Leave to set.

*9*  Serve or store in an airtight container for up to a week.

# MILLIONAIRE'S DEEP PAN COOKIES

## INGREDIENTS

*Makes 10*

225g (2 sticks) unsalted butter

170g (¾ cup plus 2 tbsp packed) light soft brown sugar

210g (generous 1 cup) caster sugar

1 tsp vanilla extract (optional)

2 eggs

50g (2½ tbsp) golden syrup

475g (3⅓ cups) plain flour

1 heaped tsp baking powder

150g (5½oz) white chocolate chips, plus extra for topping

150g (5½oz) milk chocolate chips, plus extra for topping

**Caramel**

90g (5½ tbsp) unsalted butter

40g (3½ tbsp) caster sugar

60g (⅓ cup) golden syrup

½ x 397g (14oz) can of condensed milk

**Topping**

300g (10oz) milk chocolate

20ml (4 tsp) vegetable oil (optional – if you'd like a smoother cut)

## SPECIAL EQUIPMENT

Mixer

10 x 10cm (4in) cookie/crumpet rings

2 baking trays, lined

Cake release spray or homemade cake release (see page 202) (optional)

Piping bag

1 Preheat the oven to 195°C (175°C fan/385°F/Gas 5½).

2 Put the butter, both sugars and the vanilla extract, if using, into a mixer and, using the paddle attachment, cream together on a high-speed setting (or use a hand-held electric whisk). Add the eggs and golden syrup and mix on a low-speed setting. Sift in the flour and baking powder. Mix together until combined.

3 Add the chocolate chips and mix again. If the dough is too sticky, you may need to add up to an extra 50g (⅓ cup) of flour.

4 Set out five cookie/crumpet rings on each lined baking tray. If using cake release spray or cake release, use on the inside of the rings.

5 Use an ice-cream scoop to pick up mixture and weigh out portions about 140–145g (5oz). Roll each one into a ball and place in the middle of a ring. Flatten slightly with your hand.

6 Add extra chocolate chips to the tops and bake for 14 minutes, or until the tops of the cookies are golden brown. Remove from the oven and drop or bang the baking trays on a hard surface.

7 Leave the cookies to cool in the rings, on the trays.

### To make the caramel

8 To make the caramel, melt the butter in a saucepan on the hob. Add the sugar and golden syrup over a low heat and stir. Pour in the condensed milk and turn up the heat. Bring to the boil while stirring continuously – you must stir vigorously or black lumps of burnt caramel will surface.

9 Once boiling, turn down the heat and stir until thickened and golden brown. Do not leave unattended – you must stir continuously. The longer you stir the caramel, the darker and richer it will become. This may take 15–20 minutes. ▶

★ If the caramel is "greasy" or the butter has started to separate, add a few teaspoons of boiling water and mix until it comes back together. We prefer to use a mixer for this, especially if you are making a large quantity, however, you can do it by hand.

★ If the caramel is left to set before putting on the cookies, it can be gently reheated and mixed with a splash of boiling water. If the caramel has set too hard, add some more butter into the mixture to retain its softness.

★ Experiment with designs or patterns – feather some white chocolate into the milk chocolate while the cookies are still in their rings.

## To finish

**10** When the cookies have cooled, spoon 1 heaped tablespoon of caramel onto each one and smooth down using the back of the spoon. Leave to set slightly in or out of the fridge.

**11** For the topping, melt the milk chocolate (and oil, if using) over a bain-marie or in a heatproof bowl in the microwave and spoon 2–3 tablespoons directly on top of the caramel and cookies, still in their rings. Use a spoon to push the chocolate up to the sides of the ring if needed. The whole cookie should be completely covered in chocolate.

**12** Leave to set, then carefully push the cookies out of the rings. Use the excess milk chocolate to decorate – load it into a piping bag, snip off the end and finely drizzle over the top.

**13** Serve or store in an airtight container for up to a week.

# S'MORES DEEP PAN COOKIES

## INGREDIENTS

*Makes 10*

225g (2 sticks) unsalted butter

170g (¾ cup plus 2 tbsp packed) light soft brown sugar

210g (generous 1 cup) caster sugar

3 tsp ground sweet cinnamon

2 eggs

50g (2½ tbsp) golden syrup

475g (3⅓ cups) plain flour

1 heaped tsp baking powder

350g (12oz) milk or dark chocolate chips

A handful of mini marshmallows

**Topping**

150g (5½oz) milk chocolate spread or milk chocolate, melted

100g (2 cups) mini marshmallows

20g (¾oz) milk or dark chocolate, melted

2 digestive biscuits, crushed

Cinnamon sugar (optional)

## SPECIAL EQUIPMENT

Mixer

10 x 10cm (4in) cookie/crumpet rings

2 baking trays, lined

Cake release spray or homemade cake release (see page 202) (optional)

Kitchen blowtorch (optional)

*1* Preheat the oven to 195°C (175°C fan/385°F/Gas 5½).

*2* Put the butter and both sugars into a mixer and, using the paddle attachment, cream together on a high-speed setting (or use a hand-held electric whisk). Add the cinnamon, eggs and golden syrup and mix on a low-speed setting. Sift in the flour and baking powder. Mix together until combined.

*3* Add the chocolate chips and marshmallows and mix again. If the dough is too sticky, you may need to add up to an extra 50g (⅓ cup) of flour.

*4* Set out five cookie/crumpet rings on each lined baking tray. If using cake release spray or cake release, use on the inside of the rings.

*5* Use an ice-cream scoop to pick up mixture and weigh out portions about 135–140g (5oz). Roll each one into a ball and place in the middle of a ring. Flatten slightly with your hand.

*6* Bake for 14 minutes, or until the tops of the cookies are golden brown. Remove from the oven and drop or bang the baking trays on a hard surface.

*7* Leave the cookies to cool in the rings, on the trays. When they have partially cooled, push out of the rings and leave to cool completely.

*8* Spread 1 teaspoon of milk chocolate spread or melted chocolate onto each cookie and top with around 10g (¼oz) mini marshmallows per cookie.

*9* Place the cookies under a hot grill for a few seconds at a time, or torch using a blowtorch if you have one. Finish with a drizzle of melted chocolate, some crushed digestives and a dusting of cinnamon sugar, if you like. Leave to cool a little or completely, then serve or store in an airtight container for up to a week.

# PEANUT BUTTER, CARAMEL & DARK CHOCOLATE COOKIE SLICE

Controversial flavours are the theme here – peanut butter and dark chocolate. We love combining saltiness with bitter dark chocolate and balancing it with sweet caramel to find the perfect balance. We appreciate peanut butter isn't for everyone, so this recipe is easily adapted to change the flavour.

## INGREDIENTS

*Makes 8–10*

160g (1¼ sticks) unsalted butter

270g (1⅓ cups) light soft brown sugar

1 egg

40g (2 tbsp) golden syrup

270g (2 cups) plain flour

1 tsp baking powder

140g (5oz) dark chocolate chips

### Decoration

20g (¾oz) salted peanuts

150g (5½oz) caramel (see page 21 or use store-bought caramel sauce)

75g (2¾oz) dark chocolate

### Peanut butter ganache

70ml (4½ tbsp) double cream

210g (7½oz) white chocolate

50g (scant ¼ cup) smooth peanut butter

## SPECIAL EQUIPMENT

Mixer or hand-held electric whisk

23cm (9in) square tin or 20 x 30cm (8 x 12in) rectangular tin, lined

Piping bags and medium open star nozzle

1  Preheat the oven to 195°C (175°C fan/385°F/Gas 5½).

2  Cream together the butter and sugar, then add the egg and golden syrup and mix. Sift in the flour and baking powder and mix until a dough forms. Add the dark chocolate chips and mix.

3  Take the dough from the mixer and knead with your hands a few times. If the dough is too sticky, add a little bit more flour. Place the dough into the lined tin and push down evenly, making sure the corners are as thick as the centre. Bake for 25 minutes, or until the top is golden brown. Cool in the tin, then chill in the fridge for several hours. Cut into 8–10 equal-sized slices.

4  Mix the peanuts with a spoonful of caramel in a heatproof bowl and place in the microwave for 5-10 seconds until melted. Leave to cool.

5  Melt the dark chocolate in a bain-marie or in short bursts in the microwave, then heap a little spoonful onto each cookie slice. When set, add a small spoonful of caramel on top.

6  To make the ganache, heat the double cream in a heatproof bowl set over a pan of simmering water, then add the white chocolate and stir. Alternatively, the cream and chocolate can be heated together in the microwave for a minute or so at a time, then mixed until smooth. Leave to set and cool, then chill in the fridge.

7  When set but soft (you should be able to put your finger through it), place in a mixer with the whisk attachment, set to a medium speed and whip before adding the peanut butter. Whipped ganache can be easily piped, so load a piping bag with the nozzle and go! It can start to solidify, so work quickly.

8  Pipe a line of peanut butter ganache on top of the chocolate and caramel. Top with a sprinkle of the caramel-covered peanuts and finish with a drizzle of the remaining melted dark chocolate.

# M&M WHITE CHOCOLATE CHEESECAKE COOKIE SLICE

We imagine these brightly coloured cheesecake cookies taking centre stage on a spread of Finch Bakery delights at a child's birthday party. Or your 30th. Just saying.

## INGREDIENTS

*Serves 9*

### Cookie base

160g (1¼ sticks) unsalted butter

270g (1⅓ cups) light soft brown sugar

1 egg

40g (2 tbsp) golden syrup

270g (2 cups) plain flour

1 tsp baking powder

140g (5oz) white chocolate chunks

100g (3½oz) chocolate M&Ms, plus extra for topping

### White chocolate cheesecake

200g (7oz) white chocolate

340g (11½oz) full-fat cream cheese

65g (½ cup) icing sugar

A dash of lemon juice

Vanilla extract, to taste

200ml (scant 1 cup) double cream

### Decoration

25g (scant 1oz) chocolate M&Ms, partially crushed

10g (2 tsp) rainbow sprinkles

## SPECIAL EQUIPMENT

Mixer or hand-held electric whisk

23cm (9in) square tin or 20 x 30cm (8 x 12in) rectangular tin, lined

Piping bag and a large open star nozzle

*1* To make the white chocolate cheesecake filling, melt the white chocolate in a heatproof bowl in the microwave or over a bain-marie. Leave to cool, but not re-solidify. Whisk together the cream cheese, icing sugar, lemon juice and vanilla extract in a bowl for 1 minute until thickened. Add the cooled white chocolate and whip again until incorporated.

*2* In a separate bowl, whip the cream until stiff but not hard. Gently fold the cream into the cream cheese mixture using a spatula. Chill in the fridge for several hours, preferably overnight, to set.

*3* To make the M&M cookie base, preheat the oven to 195°C (175°C fan/385°F/Gas 5½).

*4* Cream together the butter and sugar, then add the egg and golden syrup and mix together. Sift in the flour and baking powder and mix until a dough forms. Add the chocolate chunks and M&Ms and mix very gently until evenly distributed.

*5* Take the dough from the mixer and knead with your hands a few times. If the dough is too sticky, add a little bit more flour. Place the dough into the lined tin and push down evenly, making sure the corners are as thick as the centre. Bake for 25 minutes, or until the top is golden brown. Cool in the tin, then either chill in the fridge for several hours until you are ready to serve or remove and cut into 9 equal-sized squares.

*6* Load the cheesecake into a piping bag fitted with a large open star nozzle and pipe a large whip of cheesecake on top of each square, before topping with more whole M&Ms, the crushed M&Ms and rainbow sprinkles.

**TOP TIP** ★ We use bake-stable white chocolate chunks to prevent them melting in the cookie base.

# SLICE & BAKE COOKIE DOUGH

Have you ever had a craving for ONE cookie but don't want to make a full batch? These cookies are rolled up and put in the freezer, ready to slice off and bake from frozen whenever you fancy. Add different toppings before going into the oven to change up the flavour! Perfect for a party of one, or if you have a couple of mates coming round for a brew.

## INGREDIENTS

*Makes 10–12*

**Vanilla cookie**

100g (6½ tbsp) unsalted butter

50g (¼ cup) caster sugar

70g (⅓ cup plus 1 tbsp packed) light soft brown sugar

1 egg

200g (scant 1½ cups) plain flour

1 tsp baking powder

½ tsp salt

1 tsp vanilla extract

100g (3½oz) milk chocolate chunks

**Chocolate cookie**

100g (6½ tbsp) unsalted butter

50g (¼ cup) caster sugar

45g (½ cup packed) light soft brown sugar

1 egg

1 tsp baking powder

½ tsp salt

150g (1 cup plus 2 tbsp) plain flour

40g (3 tbsp) cocoa powder

100g (3½oz) white chocolate chunks

## SPECIAL EQUIPMENT

Mixer or hand-held electric whisk

Baking tray, lined

1  To make the vanilla cookie, cream together the butter and both sugars, then add the egg.

2  Sift in the flour, baking powder and salt, then add the vanilla extract and mix until a dough forms. Add the milk chocolate chunks and mix until evenly distributed. Wrap the dough in cling film and place in the fridge to firm up.

3  Follow steps 1–2 using the ingredients for the chocolate cookies, adding the cocoa powder with the dry ingredients. Wrap the dough in cling film and place in the fridge to firm up.

4  Once both doughs are firm, roll out each one into a rectangle about 20 x 30cm (8 x 12in).

5  Place one rectangle onto a piece of cling film and place onto a lined baking tray.

6  Carefully place the other cookie layer over the first so they are laying flat. Place the baking tray against the kitchen wall on the work surface and use your hands and the cling film to manipulate the cookie into a roll. The cling film can be removed; however, it may also be used as a tool to help achieve a tighter roll, using the baking tray against the wall as leverage.

7  Wrap tightly in cling film and freeze for up to 3 months.

8  Remove from the freezer as and when needed and use a sharp knife to cut off a section of cookie dough – depending on how thick you'd like the cookie(s), this should make 10-12 slices. Bake from frozen on a lined baking tray at 180°C (160°C fan/350°F/Gas 4) for 18 minutes. Leave to cool on the tray.

**TOP TIPS** ★ Use bake-stable chocolate chunks to ensure they don't melt while in the oven. ★ Add your favourite toppings (we like sprinkles, M&Ms, Ferrero Rocher, Creme Eggs or small pieces of chocolate) to change the flavour (some may burn in the oven, so add after baking while still warm).

# CELEBRATION CAKES

# CARAMEL LATTE CAKE

Coffee lovers unite! A beautiful coffee cake layered between a caramel and creamy buttercream filling, this caffeinated treat will certainly hit the spot, any time of the day.

## INGREDIENTS

*Makes a 20cm (8in), 4-layer cake*

600g (5 sticks) unsalted butter

600g (3 cups) caster sugar

2–3 tbsp fine instant coffee

10 eggs

600g (4⅔ cups) self-raising flour

### Filling

500g (4 sticks plus 2 tbsp) unsalted butter

1–2 tbsp fine instant coffee

800g (6⅔ cups) icing sugar

150ml (⅔ cup) double cream

200g (½ cup) caramel (see page 21 or use store-bought caramel)

### Decoration

Chocolate coffee cups (optional, see page 39)

500g (4 sticks plus 2 tbsp) unsalted butter

900g (7½ cups) icing sugar

Vanilla extract, to taste

2–3 tbsp fine instant coffee

A couple of squares of white chocolate

Edible gold leaf

Coffee beans

## SPECIAL EQUIPMENT

2 (360ml/12fl oz) paper coffee cups, lids and paper straws

Mixer or hand-held electric whisk

4 x 20cm (8in) cake tins, lined

Piping bag(s) and open star nozzle

28cm (11in) cake drum, turntable and dowels (optional)

Straight-edge scraper

*1* Follow the method on page 39 to make the edible chocolate coffee cups, if using. Leave to set.

*2* Preheat the oven to 180°C (160°C fan/350°F/Gas 4).

*3* Cream the butter and sugar together on a high-speed setting in your mixer. Boil the kettle and add 1 tablespoon of boiling water to the instant coffee. Add the eggs to the butter/sugar mixture, one by one, on a low-speed setting, until just combined. Sift in the flour, add the liquid coffee and mix slowly. Scrape down the sides of the bowl with a spatula. Mix until combined.

*4* Weigh 550g (1lb 4oz) of batter into each lined tin. Bake for 30 minutes, or until the sponges bounce back when pressed or a cocktail stick inserted into the centres comes out clean.

*5* Take the cakes out of the tins and leave to cool completely on wire racks. If decorating straight away, trim the top of the cakes with a knife or cake leveller until flat.

### Filling and stacking

*6* Prepare the coffee buttercream for the filling by creaming the butter for at least 10 minutes. Meanwhile, boil the kettle again and add 1 teaspoon of boiling water to the instant coffee. When the butter is whitened and doubled in size, sift in half the icing sugar and mix on a low-speed setting. Once just combined, add the remaining icing sugar, the coffee paste and double cream. Combine on a high-speed setting for a further 5 minutes. If too soft, put in the fridge for 5 minutes to firm up.

*7* Load a piping bag with the coffee buttercream and stick one sponge down onto the cake drum. Pipe rings around the edge of this sponge and another two sponges. Use a spoon to spread some caramel onto the sponges, carefully pushing it right up to the buttercream rings. Chill in the freezer (or fridge) until the rings are solid. ▶

**8**  Evenly distribute the coffee buttercream over the top of the caramel on the bottom sponge and smooth over with an angled spatula. Stack and repeat with the next two sponge layers (you will now have three sponge layers stacked and filled). For the final sponge, flip it upside down so the top is flat. Chill in the fridge for 30 minutes.

**9**  Meanwhile, make the buttercream to decorate by whipping the butter for 10 minutes. Add half the icing sugar and the vanilla extract and slowly mix until just combined. Add the rest of the icing sugar and mix on a low-speed setting until combined. Use the back of a spatula to smooth the buttercream and pop any air bubbles. Set about one quarter of the vanilla buttercream aside, then mix the coffee into the main buttercream.

**10**  Crumb coat the cake (see page 209). Use an angled spatula to roughly apply the coffee buttercream to the sides and top of the cake and use a straight-edge scraper to remove the excess. Chill until ready to decorate.

### Decoration

**11**  Pipe the coffee buttercream directly onto the crumb-coated cake using a piping bag with a snipped top. Use a straight-edge scraper to pull around the cake until the buttercream is smooth and flat. Chill for 15 minutes.

**12**  Loosen the remaining caramel in the microwave for the drip. Add a couple of squares of white chocolate to the caramel and stir until melted together – this should give stability to the drip. Use a spoon to guide the caramel drips over the edge of the cake. When partially dried and still tacky, push some pieces of edible gold leaf into the drip. Chill until the caramel has solidified.

**13**  While the cake is chilling, put the reserved vanilla buttercream into a piping bag with any open star nozzle. Pipe small drop stars onto the top of the cake and around the base. Fill the chocolate coffee cups with buttercream and drizzle over some caramel. Arrange the filled chocolate coffee cups on top of the cake. Decorate the buttercream with coffee beans.

# LATTE CHEESECAKE COFFEE CUPS

One day we saw a chocolate coffee cup on Instagram... so we had to make a chocolate coffee cup (and fill it with cheesecake!). This simple but effective creation can be filled with almost anything.

## INGREDIENTS

*Makes 2*

**For the cups**

300g (10oz) white chocolate

50g (1¾oz) milk chocolate

Splash of vegetable oil

**For the cheesecake**

150ml (⅔ cup) double cream

1 tbsp fine instant coffee

250g (9oz) full-fat cream cheese

80g (6½ tbsp) caster sugar

**For the biscuit base**

100g (3½oz) digestive biscuits

50g (1¾oz) unsalted butter

**Decoration (optional)**

Cocoa powder, for dusting

Caramel (see page 21 or use store-bought caramel sauce)

## SPECIAL EQUIPMENT

2 (360ml/12fl oz) paper coffee cups, lids and paper straws

Mixer or hand-held electric whisk

Piping bag and open star nozzle (optional)

*1* First, make the biscuit base by blitzing the digestive biscuits in a food processor, or put them in a sandwich bag and crush with a rolling pin.

*2* Melt the unsalted butter and pour into the biscuits, stirring to coat them all. Set aside.

*3* Temper the white chocolate following the instructions on page 216. Temper the milk chocolate and stir into the white chocolate slightly until marbled.

*4* Pour the chocolate into one coffee cup and tip the cup up slightly so the chocolate coats the top, up to the rim. Leave for a couple of minutes, then repeat with the second cup. Repeat 3–4 times for each cup.

*5* In between pouring the chocolate, prepare the cheesecake. Using a mixer or hand-held electric whisk, slowly whip the double cream until stiff.

*6* In a separate bowl, measure out the instant coffee and pour in a dash of boiling water. Add the cream cheese and caster sugar and beat together until fluffy. Start to fold in the whipped cream with a spatula while slowly adding the excess chocolate from the coffee cups (about 200g/7oz). Mix until just combined.

*7* Once completely set, cut around the bottom of the coffee cups with scissors and carefully peel away the paper from the chocolate. You may need to use a knife to pick away at the seam in the paper cups. Unravel the paper and discard.

*8* Layer the biscuit base alternately with the cheesecake in the chocolate coffee cups, using a rolling pin to gently push the biscuit layer down if needed. Using a palette knife (or a loaded piping bag with an open star nozzle), create a whip on top of each cup with the remaining cheesecake. Dust with cocoa powder and add a drizzle of caramel, if you like. Sprinkle over the remaining crumbs of the biscuit base and add a chunky straw to each cup.

600g (5 sticks) unsalted butter

600g (3 cups) caster sugar

10 eggs

15–20 drops of lemon extract

100g (3½oz) poppy seeds

600g (4⅔ cups) self-raising flour

### Filling

250g (2 sticks) unsalted butter

Lemon extract, to taste

400g (3⅓ cups) icing sugar

About 150g (5½oz) lemon curd

### Decoration

500g (4 sticks plus 2 tbsp) unsalted butter

800g (6⅔ cups) icing sugar, sifted

Lemon extract, to taste

Pink gel food colouring

Lilac gel food colouring

Yellow gel food colouring

Orange gel food colouring

Mint-green gel food colouring

Mini Eggs

Sprinkles

## SPECIAL EQUIPMENT

Mixer or hand-held electric whisk

4 x 20cm (8in) cake tins, lined

Cake leveller (optional)

Piping bag, open and closed star and flat ribbon nozzles

28cm (11in) cake drum, turntable and dowels (optional)

Straight-edge scraper

# LEMON POPPY SEED LAMBETH CAKE

**Lambeth cakes are bang on trend and a great way to practise and show off your piping skills! This lemon poppy seed cake would be a fabulous addition to a spring BBQ.**

*1*   Preheat the oven to 180°C (160°C fan/350°F/Gas 4).

*2*   Beat the butter and sugar until whitened, then crack the eggs into a bowl. Reduce to a low-speed setting, then slowly add the eggs. Add the lemon extract and poppy seeds. Sift in the flour and fold in with a spatula until just combined.

*3*   Weigh out about 500g (1lb 2oz) of cake batter evenly into each lined tin. Bake for 30–35 minutes, or until the sponges bounce back when pressed. Leave to cool in the tins for 10 minutes, then turn out onto wire racks and leave to cool completely.

### Filling and stacking

*4*   Use a cake leveller or a knife to evenly trim the top of each sponge.

*5*   In a mixer, whip together the butter and lemon extract until whitened and doubled in size. Sift in the icing sugar and combine on a low-speed setting until just combined. Scrape around the sides of the bowl with a spatula and mix again. Load into a piping bag and snip off the end.

*6*   Use buttercream to stick down one sponge onto the cake drum. Pipe a thick line around the edge and spoon in some lemon curd, pushing it evenly up to the edge with a spoon. Repeat on two more of the sponges and freeze for 10 minutes, or chill in the fridge for 30 minutes.

*7*   Once hardened, pipe more lemon buttercream over the top of the lemon curd and smooth out using an angled spatula. Stack the cake, with the final layer, turned upside down to achieve a flat top. Chill for 15 minutes before using more buttercream to crumb coat the cake (see page 209). Save any excess buttercream for later and chill the cake until you are ready to decorate. ▶

### Decoration

**8** Cream the butter in a mixer on a high-speed setting for 10 minutes. Add half the icing sugar and slowly mix until combined, then add the remaining icing sugar. Add the lemon extract and mix in the leftover buttercream from the filling.

**9** Divide the buttercream between five different bowls, leaving the majority in one bowl. Colour the largest (majority) portion pale pink with the gel food colouring and apply it to the sides and top of the cake with an angled spatula. Smooth with a straight-edge scraper and use a smaller angled spatula to flatten the top. Return the cake to the fridge for 1 hour.

**10** For this cake we have used pink, lilac, yellow, orange and mint. Use a small amount of colouring for each buttercream so you can build up the colour by adding more if you need to.

**11** Load four piping bags with different nozzles – we used small and medium closed star nozzles, plus small open star and flat ribbon nozzles. With this type of cake you can use multiple nozzles or only a couple to make different effects, so go wild and use pretty much any you like!

**12** You can measure out the loops on your cake with a cookie cutter, drinking glass or just do it freehand. Follow the lines of the cookie cutter to create a ruffle. Pipe directly over the top for a double ruffle, creating a draped look.

**13** Using the rest of the nozzles, use rope and shell (see page 205) buttercream effects as well as more ruffles and rosettes.

**14** Finish the cake with Mini Eggs and sprinkles of your choice.

# NUTELLA CAKE

Who doesn't adore Nutella? Four layers of chocolate sponge sandwiched with Nutella filling and buttercream adorned with hazelnut chocolates – you won't want to cut this cake!

## INGREDIENTS

*Makes a 20cm (8in), 4-layer cake*

600g (5 sticks) unsalted butter

600g (3 cups) caster sugar

10 eggs

500g (3½ cups) self-raising flour

100g (1 cup) cocoa powder

80ml (5 tbsp) vegetable oil

### Filling

250g (2 sticks) unsalted butter

400g (3⅓ cups) icing sugar

200g (¾ cup plus 1 tbsp) softened Nutella, plus about 300g (1¼ cups)

### Decoration

500g (4 sticks plus 2 tbsp) unsalted butter

780g (6⅓ cups) icing sugar

20g (¼ cup) cocoa powder, plus extra for a darker colour

50g (1¾oz) milk chocolate spread or milk chocolate

A dash of vegetable oil

Chopped hazelnuts

Ferrero Rocher

Gold lustre spray

Kinder Bueno, broken into pieces

Kinder Chocolates, broken into pieces

## SPECIAL EQUIPMENT

4 x 20cm (8in) cake tins, lined

28cm (11in) cake drum, turntable and dowels (optional)

Piping bags and any open star nozzle

Straight-edge scraper

Micro bubble scraper

1  Preheat the oven to 180°C (160°C fan/350°F/Gas 4).

2  Put the butter and sugar into the bowl of a mixer (or use a mixing bowl and a hand-held electric whisk). Using the paddle attachment, cream together on a high-speed setting until combined and pale in colour. Add the eggs, one by one, on a medium speed setting. Scrape down the sides with a spatula and re-mix.

3  Sift in the flour and cocoa powder and add the oil. Mix again on a low-speed setting, remembering to scrape down the sides of the bowl with a spatula to catch any congealed egg. Do not overmix.

4  Evenly pour the batter into each lined tin (about 500g/1lb 2oz in each) and bake for 30–35 minutes, or until the sponges bounce back when pressed. Leave to cool in the tins for 10 minutes, then turn out onto wire racks and leave to cool completely.

### Filling and stacking

5  For the filling, make a batch of **PLAIN BUTTERCREAM** (see page 200) using the quantities listed here, adding the 200g (¾ cup plus 1 tbsp) of softened Nutella.

6  Level and stack the cake (see pages 206–207), using more softened Nutella and the Nutella buttercream as the filling.

7  Chill the cake for 15–30 minutes until solid. Crumb coat (see page 209) with the remaining buttercream and return to the fridge for another 30 minutes, or up to a week. ▶

## Decoration

**8**  Prepare a batch of **CHOCOLATE BUTTERCREAM** (see page 200) using the quantities listed on page 45. Load a piping bag and snip off the end. Follow the ombre buttercream technique on page 213, adding more cocoa powder into the buttercream before applying each layer. Scrape round with a straight-edge scraper until smooth, then finish with a textured scraper – we used a micro bubble scraper for this cake.

**9**  Apply a milk chocolate drip of your choice (see page 214). When partially dried and still tacky, push some chopped hazelnuts into the drip. Leave to set.

**10**  Load the remaining buttercream into a piping bag with an open star nozzle. Cover the top of the cake using a rosette technique (see page 204).

**11**  Spray Ferrero Rocher with gold lustre spray and arrange on top of the cake. Fill in the rest of the cake top with pieces of Kinder Bueno and Chocolates. Sprinkle with more chopped hazelnuts and chill for 30 minutes or until the day of cutting.

> **TOP TIP** ★ Nutella doesn't work well melted and used as a drip as the texture is too thick. Try another hazelnut milk chocolate spread instead.

# RAINBOW DISCO CAKE

This cake doesn't need an introduction – from the striking black buttercream to the rainbow surprise, it wouldn't look out of place at any occasion (and would be a guaranteed talking point too!).

## INGREDIENTS

*Makes a 20cm (8in), 7-layer cake*

800g (6 sticks plus 6 tbsp) unsalted butter

800g (4 cups) caster sugar

12 eggs

800g (5¾ cups) self-raising flour

Red, orange, yellow, green, blue, indigo and violet gel food colourings

### Vanilla buttercream

250g (2 sticks) unsalted butter

400g (3⅓ cups) icing sugar

Vanilla extract, to taste

### Decoration

500g (4 sticks plus 2 tbsp) unsalted butter

Black gel food colouring

900g (7½ cups) icing sugar

Vanilla extract, to taste

50g (1¾oz) milk chocolate or milk chocolate spread

A dash of vegetable oil

Black oil-based food colouring

Colourful sprinkles

## SPECIAL EQUIPMENT

Mixer or hand-held electric whisk

7 bowls and spoons

7 x 20cm (8in) cake tins, lined

28cm (11in) cake drum, turntable and dowels (optional)

Piping bags and any open star nozzle, plus a drop star nozzle

Straight-edge scraper

12cm (4½in) thin cake card

Disco balls (available online)

*1* Preheat the oven to 180°C (160°C fan/350°F/Gas 4).

*2* Cream the butter and sugar together using a mixer until light and fluffy. When combined, add the eggs, one by one, on a low-speed setting.

*3* Sift in the flour and combine on a low-speed setting (or with a spatula by hand) – it is important not to overmix.

*4* Weigh out about 280g (9⅓oz) of batter into each bowl. Depending on the brand of food colouring you are using, add a small amount at a time to each bowl and carefully fold in with a spatula until you have your desired colours.

*5* Spoon each coloured batter into a lined tin. Bake for 25-30 minutes, or until the sponges bounce back when pressed. Leave to cool in the tins for 5–10 minutes, then turn out onto wire racks and leave to cool completely.

### Filling and stacking

*6* Make a batch of **VANILLA BUTTERCREAM** (see page 200 for method) using the quantities listed here and adding vanilla extract to taste.

*7* Level and stack the cake (see pages 206–207). For a rainbow cake we use no filling – just buttercream.

*8* Chill the cake in the fridge for 15 minutes before crumb coating with the remaining buttercream (see page 209). Chill for a further 15–30 minutes or until you are ready to decorate. ▶

## Decoration

**9** To prepare the black buttercream, whip the butter until fluffy and whitened. Add 1 teaspoon of black food colouring and continue to mix. Add half the icing sugar and mix on a low-speed setting until just combined, then add the remaining half. Scrape down the sides of the bowl with a spatula, add the vanilla extract and mix again. If the black buttercream is still quite grey, add another teaspoon of colouring. (See Tips.) If the buttercream is too loose, chill in the fridge for a further 10 minutes before mixing with the mixer again.

**10** Take the cake out of the fridge and place onto a turntable. With a piping bag with the end snipped off, apply the buttercream to the outside of the cake and a layer on the top. Use a straight-edge scraper to scrape over the buttercream, saving the excess in the bowl. Scrape around the cake until the buttercream is smooth with even sides. Use an angled spatula to flatten the buttercream on the top and put back into the fridge to chill for 15 minutes.

**11** While the cake is chilling, choose a milk chocolate drip technique (see page 214) and use the black oil-based food colouring to turn the milk chocolate black.

**12** Add a small, thin cake card to the top of the cake. Cover in a small amount of black buttercream and position the disco balls on top.

**13** Use a spoon to guide the chocolate drip over the edge of the cake. Leave to set, then load a piping bag with the remaining black buttercream and fit with a drop star nozzle. Pipe onto the top and around the base of the cake, adding plenty of sprinkles for a pop of colour.

**14** Cut into the cake for a rainbow surprise!

**TOP TIPS** ★ For vibrant colours without compromising the texture of the sponge, we use gel food colouring. ★ To intensify the black buttercream, once very dark grey, blast the buttercream in the microwave for 10 seconds and then chill in the fridge for 10 minutes. Keep repeating until black! The depth of colour of the buttercream will also continue to develop on the cake. ★ Unless the disco balls are food grade, they should not touch the cake. We used a small, thin, cake card to prevent this.

## INGREDIENTS

*Makes a 20cm (8in), 4-layer cake*

600g (5 sticks) unsalted butter

600g (3 cups) caster sugar

10 eggs

600g (4⅔ cups) plain flour

**Filling**

750g (6 sticks plus 2 tbsp) unsalted butter

10 drops of vanilla extract (or to taste)

1.3kg (generous 10 cups) icing sugar

Pink, orange, yellow, green, blue, indigo and violet gel food colourings

**Decoration**

500g (4 sticks plus 2 tbsp) unsalted butter

10 drops of vanilla extract (or to taste)

800g (6⅔ cups) icing sugar, sifted

200–300g (7–10oz) sprinkles, plus extra to decorate

10g (2 tsp) whitening powder (optional)

2 tbsp white chocolate spread

Pink oil-based food colouring

Edible silver leaf

Candles

## SPECIAL EQUIPMENT

Mixer or hand-held electric whisk

4 x 20cm (8in) cake tins, lined

28cm (11in) cake drum, turntable and dowels (optional)

Straight-edge scraper

Piping bags and open star nozzles

# RAINBOW SPRINKLE BIRTHDAY CAKE

**This cake is as fun to make as it is to look at! Perfect for creating with children – although they might not want to help with the washing up! This is the most fabulous pastel birthday cake for children and adults alike.**

*1*    Preheat the oven to 180°C (160°C fan/350°F/Gas 4).

*2*    Put the butter and sugar into a mixer and, using the paddle attachment, cream together on a high-speed setting (or use a hand-held electric whisk). Reduce to a low-speed setting and add the eggs, one by one. Sift in the flour, then gradually fold in with a spatula or on a low-speed setting until just combined.

*3*    Pour about 500g (1lb 2oz) of batter evenly into each lined tin. Bake for 30–35 minutes, or until the sponges bounce back when pressed. Leave to cool in the tins for 10 minutes, then turn out onto wire racks and leave to cool completely.

### Filling and stacking

*4*    Make a batch of **VANILLA BUTTERCREAM** (see page 200 for method) using the quantities listed here.

*5*    Divide the buttercream into 7 bowls and use gel food colouring to create one pastel colour per bowl.

*6*    Use a cake leveller or a sharp knife to carefully trim the tops of the cakes. Next, cut each layer in half so you have 8 thin cake layers. Use some buttercream to stick one sponge onto the cake drum and fill each layer with the correct coloured buttercream, working backwards up the rainbow by starting with violet and finishing with pink. Save 1 tablespoon of each colour buttercream to use later. Chill in the fridge for 15 minutes.
▶

### Decoration

**7** To make the buttercream for decoration, whip the butter for 10 minutes until doubled in volume. Add the vanilla extract and half the icing sugar, combining on a low-speed setting. Add the remaining icing sugar and mix to combine.

**8** Use a thin layer of buttercream to cover the cake for a crumb coat (see page 209). Chill for 30 minutes.

**9** Once hardened, apply the buttercream to the sides and the top of the cake before using a straight-edge scraper to smooth it over. Return the cake back to the fridge for about another 30 minutes. Separate any leftover buttercream into two bowls. Add the sprinkles to one bowl and the whitening powder, if using, to the other and mix.

**10** Apply a very thin layer of sprinkle buttercream over the hardened buttercream and use the straight-edge scraper to smooth it down. You may not be able to achieve a super smooth effect if you have used quite chunky sprinkles but using boiling water to heat up the cake scraper for the final scrape will help!

**11** Add a drip of your choice (see page 214) – we used white chocolate spread, coloured pink with oil-based food colouring. When partially dried and still tacky, push some pieces of edible silver leaf into the drip. Leave to set.

**12** Transfer the plain buttercream to a piping bag with a medium open star nozzle and pipe around the base of the cake, finishing with a scattering of sprinkles.

**13** Load a piping bag with an open star nozzle and the remaining violet buttercream and pipe a small whip on top of the cake. Continue piping whips of each remaining colour (in the order of a rainbow) and finish by scattering more sprinkles on top. Add candles of your choice.

> **TOP TIP** ★ You will need flat sprinkles to achieve the look of this cake. As there is only buttercream as a filling, you may want to use more to achieve a taller cake.

# SUMMER FLORAL CAKE

This light yet moist pink sponge is laced with Champagne (or Prosecco), decorated with colourful edible flowers and finished with buttercream blooms – perfect for a summer's day celebration.

## INGREDIENTS

Makes a 20cm (8in), 3-layer cake

540g (4 sticks plus 4 tbsp) unsalted butter

650g (3¼ cups) caster sugar

9 egg whites

120ml (scant ½ cup) soured cream

250ml (generous 1 cup) Champagne or Prosecco

2 tsp vanilla extract

650g (5 cups) self-raising flour

½ tsp bicarbonate of soda

Pink gel food colouring

### Filling

250g (2 sticks) unsalted butter

450g (3¼ cups) icing sugar

50ml (3½ tbsp) Champagne or Prosecco

Vanilla extract or strawberry flavouring, to taste

Orange gel food colouring

### Decoration

500g (4 sticks plus 2 tbsp) unsalted butter

800g (6⅔ cups) icing sugar

2–3 tsp whitening powder (optional)

Vanilla extract or strawberry flavouring, to taste

Food colouring gel of your choice

Gold nonpareils

Edible flowers

## SPECIAL EQUIPMENT

Mixer or hand-held electric whisk

3 x 20cm (8in) cake tins, lined

28cm (11in) cake drum, turntable and dowels (optional)

Piping bags and nozzles

1   Preheat the oven to 180°C (160°C fan/350°F/Gas 4).

2   Put the butter and sugar into the bowl of a mixer and, using the paddle attachment, cream together on a high-speed setting (or use a mixing bowl and a hand-held electric whisk). Once the butter has turned pale, add the egg whites, one by one, on a medium speed setting. Scrape down the sides with a spatula and re-mix.

3   Combine the soured cream, Champagne and vanilla extract (the wet ingredients) in a jug. Sift the flour and bicarbonate of soda into another bowl (the dry ingredients).

4   Add about one third of the wet ingredients to the butter and sugar mixture and beat to combine, then add one third of the dry ingredients and beat again. Repeat until everything has been added, finishing with the last of the dry ingredients.

5   Add the pink colouring until your desired shade has been reached. Beat for 30 seconds until fully incorporated.

6   Divide the pink batter evenly the lined tins and bake for 35–40 minutes, or until the sponges bounce back when pressed. Leave to cool in the tins for 10 minutes, then turn out onto to wire racks and leave to cool completely.

### Filling and stacking

7   Make a batch of **PLAIN BUTTERCREAM** (see page 200) using the quantities listed here and whipping the butter for 5–10 minutes first. Add the Champagne or Prosecco and either vanilla extract or strawberry flavouring – this goes well with fizz! We also added some orange food colouring. Chill in the fridge for 30 minutes as the liquid will make the buttercream soft.

8   Level and stack the cake (see pages 206–207) using the buttercream as the filling. ▶

**9** Chill the cake for 10 minutes until solid. Crumb coat (see page 209) with the remaining buttercream and return to the fridge for another 30 minutes or until ready to decorate.

### Decoration

**10** Make a batch of **PLAIN BUTTERCREAM** (see page 200) using the quantities listed here and adding whitening powder, if using, then flavour to suit your taste. Load a piping bag and snip off the end with a pair of scissors. Apply and smooth the buttercream over the top and sides of the cake (see page 209), paying special attention to the top as this will be the focal point of the cake. Save the excess buttercream to decorate. Chill in the fridge for 1 hour.

**11** Remove the cake from the fridge and use a sharp knife to make sure the top is flat and then cut the very edge of one side of the cake off, so it can sit flat on its side. Use a cake lifter to position the cake on its new flat edge, refrigerate and then smooth more buttercream over any imperfections and the back of the cake. Use a straight-edge scraper to smooth.

**12** Use a sharp knife to carve lines into the side of the cake (which was the top) and the curved edges of the sides. These will be the stems of the buttercream flowers. Use some excess buttercream and colouring to the match theme of the cake – we have used pink and orange. Pipe a small blob of buttercream using a piping bag and gently drag into a petal shape using a palette knife, repeating in a circular pattern with five petals in total, creating a daisy. Dainty blobs and smaller palette knives will allow more delicate-looking flowers. Petal nozzles can also be used to create different flowers – go as complicated as you dare (our favourites are simple ones though). Use the gold nonpareils for the centre of the flowers.

**13** Refrigerate any leftover buttercream for a future project.

**14** Apply the edible flowers just before serving; edible flowers will stay fresh in the fridge but wilt if left out for too long, so are best added on the day of the event. Attach using a small amount of buttercream, royal icing or edible glue, using a paintbrush to smooth down any petals that stick awkwardly.

# RASPBERRY & WHITE CHOCOLATE CHEESECAKE CAKE

Decorated with ice cream cones, pastel colours and filled with white chocolate and raspberry cheesecake, this vanilla layer cake is the perfect centrepiece for a summer's day party.

## INGREDIENTS

*Makes a 20cm (8in), 4-layer cake*

- 600g (5 sticks) unsalted butter
- 600g (3 cups) caster sugar
- 10 eggs
- 600g (4⅔ cups) self-raising flour

**Filling**

- 300g (10oz) white chocolate
- 200ml (scant 1 cup) double cream
- 350g (12oz) full-fat cream cheese
- 75g (6 tbsp) caster sugar
- 150g (5½oz) raspberries
- Pink gel food colouring

**For the buttercream rings and crumb coat**

- 250g (2 sticks) unsalted butter
- 5 drops of vanilla extract, or to taste
- 400g (3⅓ cups) icing sugar, sifted

**Decoration**

- 500g (4 sticks plus 2 tbsp) unsalted butter
- 5–10 drops of vanilla extract
- 800g (6⅔ cups) icing sugar, sifted
- Pale pink oil-based food colouring
- Mint-green oil-based food colouring
- Mini cupcakes
- 200g (7oz) white chocolate
- 2 waffle ice-cream cones
- Cocktail or glacé cherries
- Pink and white chocolate shards

## SPECIAL EQUIPMENT

- Mixer or hand-held electric whisk
- 4 x 20cm (8in) cake tins, lined
- 28cm (11in) cake drum, turntable and dowels (optional)
- Piping bag and open star nozzles
- Straight-edge scraper
- 10–15 polystyrene balls (mixed sizes)
- Food-grade disco balls (available online – optional)

▶

1   Preheat the oven to 180°C (160°C fan/350°F/Gas 4).

2   In a mixer, beat the butter and sugar on a high-speed setting until whitened. Reduce to a low-speed setting and add the eggs, one by one. Sift in the flour, then fold in with a spatula, or on a low-speed setting, until just combined.

3   Pour about 500g (1lb 2oz) of batter evenly into each lined tin. Bake for 30–35 minutes, or until the sponges bounce back when pressed. Leave to cool in the tins for 10 minutes, then turn out onto to wire racks and leave to cool completely.

4   To make the cheesecake filling, melt the white chocolate in the microwave or over a bain-marie. Set aside and leave to cool completely but not solidify.

5   Whip the double cream in a mixer on a low-speed setting, gradually increasing the speed until stiff. Use a spatula to scrape into another bowl. Combine the cream cheese and sugar until thickened and then add the melted white chocolate, slowly, on a low-speed setting. Fold in the whipped cream and raspberries with a spatula.

6   Finally, add a small amount of pink food colouring and gently mix to marble. Chill in the fridge until ready to use.


### Filling and stacking

7   Trim the tops of the cakes with a knife or a cake leveller.

8   Whip the butter and vanilla extract until whitened, then add the icing sugar, 200g (1⅔ cups) at a time. Combine on a low-speed setting until just mixed together.

9   Load a piping bag with the vanilla buttercream and pipe a ring around the edge of three sponge layers.

10  Chill in the fridge for 30 minutes or the freezer for 15 minutes. This will create a dam to keep the cake stable when assembling.

11  Once hardened, add the cheesecake filling and use a spatula to evenly spread. Stack the cake and put back in the fridge for 15 minutes.

**12** With the excess buttercream, crumb coat the cake (see page 209) using a palette knife and straight-edge scraper and return to the fridge until hardened and ready to decorate. The cake can be stored for a couple of days in advance and will still stay fresh due to the crumb coat. Any leftover buttercream can be saved to decorate.

**TOP TIP** ★ Have fun with the colours! In this recipe, we dipped the ice-cream cones in the leftover tempered white chocolate.

### Decoration

**13** To make the buttercream, whip the butter and vanilla extract for 10 minutes. Add the icing sugar in two parts, mixing slowly in between until just combined. Remember to combine any leftover buttercream from the crumb coat into the bowl. Separate into two bowls and colour one pink and one mint-green.

**14** Load a piping bag with pink buttercream and apply evenly to the top and down the sides of the first quarter of the cake. Use a straight-edge scraper to smooth over the buttercream. Return to the fridge for 10 minutes and save any leftover pink buttercream.

**15** Load another piping bag with the mint-green buttercream and pipe over halfway down the pink buttercream to around a third of the way down the cake. Use a straight-edge scraper to smooth this layer and return the cake to the fridge for a further 10 minutes. Repeat until the cake is covered in alternate colours. Pipe small whips on top of the mini cupcakes and set aside.

**16** Prepare the polystyrene balls by tempering the white chocolate (see page 216) and dividing in half. Colour each half with the pink and mint-green food colourings, then use a cocktail stick to dip the balls into the chocolate. Set upright (stick into a polystyrene cake drum, oasis, even out of use blocks of butter).

**17** Use cocktail sticks to secure one waffle cone upright on one side of the cake, then trim the bottom off the other cone and place on top of the cake. Spoon the remaining cheesecake filling into the top of cones – you may need to use excess buttercream to fill the base of the cones before adding the cheesecake. Add cherries to the top. Pipe small whips of buttercream on the side of the cake around the waffle cone.

**18** Arrange the polystyrene balls, mini cupcakes and disco balls, if using, around the top and the base of the cake.

*Makes a 20cm (8in), 4-layer cake*

- 600g (5 sticks) unsalted butter
- 600g (3 cups) caster sugar
- 175ml (¾ cup) vegetable oil
- 10 eggs
- 120g (1¼ cups) black cocoa powder
- 50g (½ cup) cocoa powder
- 500g (3½ cups) self-raising flour

**Filling**

- 500g (4½ sticks) unsalted butter
- 800g (6⅔ cups) icing sugar
- Caramel flavouring, to taste
- Purple gel food colouring
- 300g (10oz) caramel
- Red gel food colouring

**Meringue ghosts**

- 2 egg whites
- 100g (½ cup) caster sugar
- Pinch of cream of tartar (optional)
- Pinch of salt
- 5 drops of vanilla extract
- Purple gel food colouring
- Small edible eyes
- Edible black food pen

**Decoration**

- 500g (4½ sticks) unsalted butter
- 800g (6⅔ cups) icing sugar
- Orange and lime-green gel food colourings
- About 20g (¾oz) milk chocolate
- Black oil-based food colouring
- Sprinkles
- Edible glitter and silver leaf

## SPECIAL EQUIPMENT

- Mixer or hand-held electric whisk
- Piping bags and open star nozzle
- 4 x 20cm (8in) cake tins, lined
- 28cm (11in) cake drum, turntable and dowels (optional)
- Straight-edge and medium-stripe scrapers

# HALLOWEEN CAKE

Complete with meringue ghosts and monsters, black drips and "slime" buttercream, turning up with this spooky cake at the Halloween disco might get you some brownie points at school!

### For the meringue ghosts and monsters

**1** Preheat the oven to 120°C (100°C fan/250°F/Gas ½).

**2** In a clean metal bowl, whisk the egg whites on a medium speed setting until foamy and doubled in size. Add the caster sugar, a spoonful at a time, then the cream of tartar and the salt and increase to a high-speed setting. The meringue should become thick, glossy and should stand up on the end of the whisk when held up. Add the vanilla extract and mix again.

**3** Load a piping bag and snip off the very end. Pipe meringue kisses on a lined baking tray by squeezing lightly and pulling up quickly – all different sizes! Mix the purple food colouring carefully into the remaining meringue, being careful not to overmix and deflate.

**4** Load a piping bag with a nozzle of your choice and pipe more purple meringue kisses onto a second lined baking tray. Bake for 1 hour, then turn off the oven and leave for another 30 minutes–1 hour.

**5** Peel off the baking parchment and use sugar paste to attach the edible eyes to the purple meringue ghosts. On the white meringue ghosts, use the edible black pen to draw on eyes and a mouth. These meringues can be made well in advance of decorating (up to 2 weeks) if stored in an airtight container.

### For the sponge

**6** Preheat the oven to 180°C (160°C fan/350°F/Gas 4).

**7** Put the butter and sugar into the bowl of a mixer (or use a mixing bowl and a hand-held electric whisk). Using the paddle attachment, cream together on a high speed. Slowly add the oil and the eggs, one by one, on a low-speed setting. Sift in both cocoa powders and the flour and combine. Remember to scrape down the sides with a spatula before re-mixing. ▶

**8**   Pour about 500g (1lb 2oz) of batter evenly into each lined tin. Bake for 30 minutes, or until the sponges bounce back when pressed. Leave to cool in the tins for 10 minutes, then turn out onto wire racks and leave to cool completely.

## Filling and stacking

**9**   Prepare the caramel buttercream (see page 200) and add the caramel flavouring to taste. Use the purple gel food colouring to colour the buttercream. Soften the caramel in the microwave and stir in some red gel food colouring to dye the caramel red.

**10**   Level and stack the cake (see pages 206–207) using the purple buttercream and red caramel as the filling. Chill the cake for 15 minutes, or until solidified. Apply the crumb coat (see page 209) and return to the fridge for 30 minutes, or until you are ready to decorate the cake. Save any leftover purple buttercream for the reverse stripe.

## Decoration

**11**   Prepare a batch of buttercream (see page 200) and divide equally between two bowls. Colour one orange and one lime-green. Load a piping bag with orange buttercream and snip the end off. Pipe directly onto the sides and top of the cake and use a straight-edge scraper to smooth. Once smooth, use a medium-stripe scraper to create grooves in the buttercream. Freeze the cake for 30 minutes, or chill in the fridge for at least 45 minutes until the buttercream has hardened.

**12**   Put the remaining purple buttercream in another piping bag and snip off the end. Fill in the grooves with the purple buttercream.

**13**   Use the straight-edge scraper to scrape around the cake, removing the excess purple buttercream. As the cake will be cold from the freezer it may take a while to scrape off the buttercream to reveal the stripes.

**14**   Trim the buttercream at the top of the cake carefully with a knife. Add a milk chocolate drip of your choice (see page 214), using the black oil-based food colouring to turn the milk chocolate black. Use a spoon to guide the drip down the sides of the cake. When partially dried and still tacky, use tweezers or a clean wet finger to apply sprinkles and edible eyes into the drip. Chill in the fridge until set.

**15**   Load a piping bag with the green buttercream and an open star nozzle and pipe whips all over the top of the cake. Decorate by arranging the meringue ghosts and monsters on top of the cake. Finish with more edible eyes, sprinkles edible glitter and silver leaf.

### TOP TIPS

★ When making the meringue, make sure the bowl is clean, as grease and water can prevent stiff peaks from forming.

★ You can either buy ready-made edible eyes from most supermarkets or make your own out of fondant.

# BLACK FOREST GATEAU

This decadent chocolate sponge could be our new favourite rich-yet-fluffy cake. Chocolate, cream and cherry is a classic flavour combination but can sometimes be seen as a bit dated. Our version tastes sublime baked into thinner layers and is dressed up as a more modern gateau with freeze-dried cherry chocolate bark and shards, edible glitter cherries and kirsch-infused whipped cream.

## INGREDIENTS

*Makes a 20cm (8in), 4-layer cake*

600g (3 cups) golden caster sugar

8 eggs

250g (1¾ cups) plain flour

½ tsp salt

1 tsp baking powder

150g (1½ cups) cocoa powder

50ml (3½ tbsp) boiling water

½ tsp espresso powder

150ml (⅔ cup) vegetable oil

400g (3 sticks plus 3 tbsp) unsalted butter, melted

### Filling

900ml (scant 4 cups) double cream

120g (scant 1 cup) icing sugar

3 tbsp kirsch, or to taste (optional)

450g (1lb) cherry conserve

50g (1¾oz) milk chocolate, grated

### Decoration

100g (3½oz) milk chocolate

100g (3½oz) dark chocolate

100g (3½oz) white chocolate

10g (¼oz) freeze-dried cherries

225g (8oz) cocktail cherries on stems, sprayed with edible glitter

## SPECIAL EQUIPMENT

Mixer or hand-held electric whisk

4 x 20cm (8in) cake tins, lined

28cm (11in) cake drum, turntable and dowels (optional)

Piping bags and large piping nozzles

Baking tray, lined

*1* Preheat the oven to 180°C (160°C fan/350°F/Gas 4).

*2* Whisk together the sugar and eggs until pale and the mixture is thick enough to leave a trail when the whisk is lifted – this may take up to 10 minutes. Sift in the flour, salt, baking and cocoa powder.

*3* Pour the boiling water into the espresso powder and leave it to dissolve. Add this, the vegetable oil and the melted butter to the batter and stir until smooth.

*4* Divide the mixture evenly between the lined tins and bake for 30–35 minutes, or until the sponges bounce back when pressed. Leave to cool in the tins for 5–10 minutes, then turn out onto wire racks and leave to cool completely.

### Filling and stacking

*5* Whisk the double cream on a low-medium speed setting until soft to stiff peaks have formed. Add the icing sugar, 1 tablespoon at a time, whisking until fully incorporated. Fold in the kirsch using a spatula, then chill in the fridge until ready to use.

*6* Stick the first layer of cake to the cake board with a little of the kirsch cream. Set one sponge aside to use as the top layer and spoon the cherry conserve into the centre of the rest of the sponge layers and spread to edge. Layer the kirsch cream on top using a palette knife. Sprinkle with some grated chocolate. Place each layer of cake on the top of the last, then sprinkle some more grated chocolate over the sides of the cake, allowing the whipped cream to catch some. Place the cake in the fridge with the leftover whipped cream, while you make the chocolate shards. Dowel the cake if required (see page 207). ▶

### Decoration

**7** Gently melt all three chocolates separately either in a bain-marie or in short bursts in the microwave. Spoon each of the chocolates onto a lined baking tray together but in random-sized spoonfuls with alternating colours. Tilt the tray in different directions until the chocolate is evenly spread.

**8** Use a skewer to feather the chocolates together and sprinkle with the crushed freeze-dried cherries. Set aside to solidify, then cut into shards while partially set for perfectly cut shapes. Leave to harden.

**9** Once the shards are solid, remove the cake from the fridge. Load the leftover whipped cream into a piping bag fiteed with a large nozzle and pipe more whips around the top of the cake. Decorate with the glittery cherries, the chocolate shards, freeze-dried cherries and the remaining grated chocolate. Chill in the fridge for a couple of hours until ready to serve. Fresh cream can be kept out of the fridge for about 4 hours, so serve before then.

# BONFIRE CAKE

You've got the gang around for fireworks in the back garden after the local bonfire, so what better way to finish the evening off than with a slice of cake (and a bonfire lolly)? This themed cake needs a bit of preparation, but the end result is flame emoji (literally).

## INGREDIENTS

*Makes a 20cm (8in), 4-layer cake*

600g (3 cups) golden caster sugar

8 eggs

600g (5 sticks) unsalted butter

500g (2 cups) golden syrup

600g (4⅔ cups) plain flour

½ tsp salt

4 tsp baking powder

½ tsp bicarbonate of soda

200ml (scant 1 cup) buttermilk

12 tbsp golden syrup (3 per sponge)

### Filling

250g (2 sticks) unsalted butter

450g (3¼ cups) icing sugar

50g (2½ tbsp) golden syrup, plus extra for drizzling

10g (½ tbsp) black treacle

### Decoration

500g (4 sticks plus 2 tbsp) unsalted butter

800g (6⅔ cups) icing sugar

Gel food colourings – navy blue, black, red, yellow and orange

Chocolate Matchmakers (any flavour)

3–4 green eating apples

50ml (3½ tbsp) water

300g (1½ cups) caster sugar

75g (⅓ cup) golden syrup

1 tsp lemon juice

100g (3½oz) white chocolate

Yellow, orange and red oil-based food colourings

Rice paper

Lollipops

Toffee popcorn

Edible gold leaf

## SPECIAL EQUIPMENT

Mixer or hand-held electric whisk

4 x 20cm (8in) cake tins, lined

28cm (11in) cake drum, turntable and dowels (optional)

Piping bags and large piping nozzles

Sugar thermometer

Lollipop sticks

Baking trays, lined

Sparkler(s) (optional)

1   Preheat the oven to 180°C (160°C fan/350°F/ Gas 4).

2   Whisk together the sugar and eggs until pale and the mixture is thick enough to leave a trail when the whisk is lifted – this may take up to 10 minutes.

3   Gently melt the butter and 500g (2 cups) of golden syrup in a pan or in short bursts in the microwave. Pour into the whipped sugar and eggs and continue to mix.

4   Sift the flour, salt, baking powder and bicarbonate of soda together into a bowl. Add one third to the wet ingredients, followed by half the buttermilk. Then add another third, followed by the remaining buttermilk and the final third of the flour mixture.

5   Divide evenly between the lined tins and bake for 45 minutes, or until the sponges bounce back when pressed. Remove from the oven and leave to cool for 5–10 minutes.

6   Heat the 12 tablespoons of golden syrup in a microwave or over a gentle heat on the hob until runny. Poke several holes in the sponges with a skewer and spoon the hot syrup over each sponge. Leave to cool completely before removing from the cake tins.

## Filling and stacking

7   Whip the butter for 5–10 minutes, then make a batch of **PLAIN BUTTERCREAM** (see page 200) using the quantities listed opposite.

8   Level and stack the cake (pages 206–207) using the plain buttercream to pipe dams, and then add the golden syrup and black treacle to the rest of the buttercream and use this as the filling.

9   Chill the cake for 10 minutes until solid. Crumb coat with the remaining buttercream

(see page 209) and return to the fridge for another 30 minutes before decorating.

## Decoration

10  Prepare a batch of **PLAIN BUTTERCREAM** (see page 200) using the quantities listed on the opposite page, then set aside about 120g (4¼oz) of buttercream to use for the flames. We have flavoured the buttercream for the outside of the cake vanilla (instead of using golden syrup or black treacle) as this will not change the colour or consistency of the buttercream.

11  Use food colouring to colour the buttercream navy blue – separate a little bit out into a bowl and add a small amount of black to the navy. This will add to the depth of the night sky.

12  Load a piping bag and snip off the end with a pair of scissors. Apply and smooth the navy buttercream over the top and sides of the cake or apply using a palette knife (see pages 209 and 210). Add in some of the navy-black buttercream towards the top of the cake and scrape. Save the excess buttercream to decorate if required. Chill in the fridge for 1 hour.

13  Divide the 120g (4¼oz) reserved plain buttercream between three bowls and colour it red, yellow and orange. Use a palette knife to gently swipe red buttercream onto the cake in an upwards motion, then chill for 10 minutes. Repeat over the top with smaller orange "flames". Chill for a further 10 minutes and finish with smaller yellow "flames".

14  Load the remaining yellow buttercream into a piping bag and cut a few millimetres off the end. Carefully pipe tiny navy and yellow dots and star shapes above the buttercream flames. Arrange some chocolate matchsticks around the buttercream flames to replicate the base of the bonfire. Chill in the fridge. ▶

**15** To make the rice paper sails, cut rice paper into the required shapes (we found ovals worked best). Place the shapes in a bowl of warm water and add some gel-based food colouring (we used three bowls with three colours). Leave the rice paper to soften (5–10 seconds), remove and then drape on a lined baking tray in different shapes. Leave to dry for several hours – depending on how wet the rice paper is this may take over 24 hours to dry.

**16** To make the candy apples, scrub the apples with water to remove any waxy coating – this will allow the sugar to stick properly.

**17** Heat the water, sugar and golden syrup in a pan over a medium heat and mix together. Add the lemon juice (this will help prevent the sugar from crystallizing) and continue to heat without stirring until the sugar syrup reaches the hard candy stage – 150°C (300°F) on a sugar thermometer.

**18** Remove from the heat and use a gel-based colouring to colour if you like (we have left ours plain, as the golden syrup gives it a lovely toffee colour already). The higher the temperature and the longer the sugar boils for, the deeper the colour and more intense the flavour will be.

**19** Remove the stalks from the apples and replace with lollipop sticks. Dip into the hot sugar and coat, then remove and place onto a lined baking tray. Some sugar may pool at the bottom, but this will give a flat bottom to place the apples upside down on top of the cake. Leave to set fully.

**20** To make the chocolate sails, melt the white chocolate gently over a bain-marie or in short bursts in the microwave. Once fully melted, split the chocolate three ways and colour yellow, orange and red using oil-based food colouring. Scrunch three pieces of baking parchment and then slightly flatten.

Pour each colour over each piece of paper, allowing the chocolate to spread over the contours of the paper. Leave to dry, then remove the paper and break pieces off to stick into the top of the cake in a flame formation.

**21** Decorate the top of the cake with swirls of buttercream, the candy apples and the chocolate and rice paper sails. We have then used bonfire lollies (on sticks and crushed), toffee popcorn, edible gold leaf and more chocolate matchsticks to complete the look. Add a sparkler or two and light them, if you wish.

### TOP TIPS

★ The outside of the sponge will be significantly darker than the inside of the sponge once baked. Don't worry – this will not compromise the cake, however, if you think the sponge is looking particularly dark, cover each tin loosely with some foil about halfway through the baking time.

★ You can make the navy buttercream a few days in advance to attain the optimum dark navy shade, however, you can also add a touch of black to your navy buttercream to achieve a deeper colour.

★ We have twisted some of the coloured rice paper sails together in order to replicate flames!

# MALTESER CHRISTMAS PUDDING CAKE

Imagine you've been given the job of making the Christmas day dessert... and then you find this recipe! With layers of chocolate cake and Irish cream liqueur buttercream, this magnificent cake doubles up as a table centrepiece that will certainly stun your family this Christmas.

## INGREDIENTS

*Serves 12–20*

400g (3 sticks plus 3 tbsp) unsalted butter

480g (scant 2½ cups) caster sugar

8 eggs

100ml (6½ tbsp) vegetable oil

330g (2⅔ cups) self-raising flour

150g (1½ cups) cocoa powder

### Buttercream

500g (4 sticks plus 2 tbsp) unsalted butter

100g (¾ cup) icing sugar

100ml (6½ tbsp) Irish cream liqueur

20g (¼ cup) cocoa powder

### Decoration

White fondant icing and green and red gel food colourings, or ready-made green and red fondant icings

Edible glue (optional)

800g (1lb 12oz) Maltesers

300g (10oz) white chocolate

## SPECIAL EQUIPMENT

Cake release spray or homemade cake release (see page 202)

2 large half-sphere cake moulds

Cake drum

Turntable

Piping bags

Dowel (optional)

Curved flexible scraper or acetate

Fondant holly stamp

1   Preheat the oven to 180°C (160°C fan/350°F/Gas 4) and use either cake release spray or homemade cake release on the inside of both half-sphere tins.

2   Cream the butter and sugar together on a high-speed setting until whitened. Crack the eggs into a jug and, one by one, slowly add to the butter and sugar mixture on a low-speed setting. Use a spatula to wipe around the bowl and mix again.

3   Pour in the oil and sift in the flour and cocoa powder. Combine again on a low-speed setting, remembering to scrape down the sides of the bowl with a spatula. Do not overmix.

4   Pour half the batter into each half-sphere tin. Bake for 1 hour, or until a skewer inserted in the middles comes out clean. Leave to cool in the tins for 5–10 minutes, then turn out onto wire racks and leave to cool completely.

### Stacking

5   While the sponges are cooling, prepare the buttercream following the instructions on page 200 using the quantities listed here and add the cream liqueur to taste. You may want to put it back into the fridge to firm up.

6   Once the sponges are cool, carefully use a knife to cut off the very end of one of the round edges of the sponge. This will create a flat surface to stick down onto the cake drum. Use a knife or a cake leveller to cut both sponges in half horizontally.

7   Load the cream liqueur buttercream into a piping bag and snip off the end. Stick the flat bottom of the cake down with buttercream and pipe a layer of buttercream on the sponge, using a palette knife to smooth it down if you wish. Add the next layer of sponge on top and repeat until the cake resembles a ball. Chill in the fridge for 15–30 minutes. If you want to add a central dowel into the cake for extra stability, follow the instructions on page 207. ▶

***8*** While the cake is chilling, sift the cocoa powder into the remaining buttercream and re-whip. Use this buttercream to apply a crumb coat to the outside of the cake (see page 209) and smooth with a curved flexible scraper or make your own with a piece of acetate. Chill for 30 minutes, or until you're ready to decorate.

***9*** While the cake is setting, prepare your fondant. Either dye white fondant icing with gel food colourings or use ready-made green and red fondant icings. Roll out the green fondant with a rolling pin and stamp out two holly leaves. Roll the red fondant into three medium-sized balls and attach to the holly leaves with edible glue or a drop of water. Set aside.

***10*** Once the cake has set, apply another layer of thick chocolate buttercream onto the cake. Gently smooth over with the scraper, acetate or a spoon – don't worry if it's not completely smooth.

***11*** Starting from the bottom, firmly push Maltesers into the buttercream. Continue adding the Maltesers in rows until you reach the top. Set in the fridge.

***12*** Temper the white chocolate (see page 216) and then gently pour over the top of the cake, letting it unevenly drip down around the sides. Leave until tacky, then arrange the fondant icing holly and berries on top.

**TOP TIP** ★ Cut a piece of acetate to create a curved scraper that will easily move around the curves of the cake. If you haven't got a scraper or acetate, use the back of a spoon!

# PUDDINGS & DESSERTS

# BISCOFF APPLE CRUMBLE

A classic with a twist! Piping hot apple crumble with a touch of Biscoff, served with custard, is a firm new favourite in our shops. This dessert would be the perfect finishing touch when entertaining on a cold winter's night.

## INGREDIENTS

*Serves 6–8*

### Filling

6 large Bramley apples

Squeeze of lemon juice

75g (5 tbsp) unsalted butter

50g (¼ cup) demerara sugar

½ tsp ground sweet cinnamon

250g (generous 1 cup) Lotus Biscoff spread

### Crumble

75g (5 tbsp) unsalted butter, cubed

125g (scant 1 cup) plain flour

½ tsp ground ginger, or to taste

125g (⅔ cup minus 2 tsp) demerara sugar

100g (3½oz) Lotus Biscoff Crumb

### Decoration (optional)

Lotus Biscoff biscuits

## SPECIAL EQUIPMENT

20 x 30cm (8 x 12in) baking tin or shallow casserole dish

*1* To make the crumble, rub the butter into the flour and ginger with your fingertips until there are small and medium chunks. Add 100g (½ cup) of the demerara sugar and lift gently with your fingers to combine – the sugar should stay whole. Add the Biscoff Crumb.

*2* Preheat the oven to 200°C (180°C fan/400°F/Gas 6).

*3* Peel the apples, if you like (leaving the skins on actually adds more flavour), core and chop into cubes, then place into a large bowl of water with the squeeze of lemon juice. This will stop them from browning.

*4* Melt 25g (scant 2 tbsp) of the butter in a large pan and add the drained apples. Shake the demerara sugar and cinnamon over the apples, stir together and put on the lid. Cook over a medium heat, stirring every couple of minutes, for 5–10 minutes until the apples are soft and slightly mushy.

*5* Melt 200g (¾ cup plus 1 tbsp) of the Biscoff spread either in the microwave or in a pan on the hob. Once liquid, pour over the apples and mix to give them a good coating.

*6* Spoon the apples into the tin and run the back of a spoon over the top to evenly spread them out. Pour the remaining 50g (¼ cup) Biscoff spread over the top of the apples.

*7* Spoon the crumble mixture over the top and sprinkle over the remaining 25g (2 tbsp) of demerara sugar.

*8* Bake for 30 minutes, or until the crumble is golden brown. The Biscoff may have started leaking out of the top.

*9* Spoon into individual bowls or pots with an extra Biscoff biscuit on top, if you like. Serve with custard or cream, or just eat straight out of the tin!

# BANOFFEE CRUMBLE

Caramel and banana is a classic combination – but does it work in crumble? Of course it does! A simple and quick recipe, perfect for using up old bananas for all you banoffee fans out there.

## INGREDIENTS

*Serves 6*

12 ripe bananas

200g (7oz) caramel (see page 21 or use store-bought caramel sauce)

30g (2½ tbsp) demerara sugar

**Crumble**

75g (5 tbsp) unsalted butter, cubed

125g (scant 1 cup) plain flour

125g (⅔ cup minus 2 tsp) demerara sugar

½ tsp ground sweet cinnamon, or to taste

½ tsp ground ginger, or to taste

**To serve**

100ml (6½ tbsp) double cream

20g (1½ tbsp) caster sugar

1 banana

20g (1 tbsp plus 2 tsp) demerara sugar

50g (1¾oz) caramel (see page 21 or use store-bought caramel sauce), melted

## SPECIAL EQUIPMENT

20 x 30cm (8 x 12in) baking tin or casserole dish

Hand-held electric whisk

1   Preheat the oven to 200°C (180°C fan/400°F/Gas 6).

2   To make the crumble, rub the butter into the flour with your fingertips until evenly distributed. Lift through the demerara sugar but do not rub it in. This will keep the crumble crunchy. Stir through the cinnamon and ginger.

3   Mash the bananas in a bowl. Leave some large and some small chunks of banana. Transfer the bananas to a pan and add 150g (5½oz) of the caramel. Stir over a medium heat until the caramel has melted into the bananas, then pour into the tin.

4   Spoon over the remaining 50g (1¾oz) of caramel and spread it out with the back of a spoon. Sprinkle over the crumble and bake for 30 minutes until golden brown.

5   While the crumble is in the oven, whip the double cream with a hand-held electric whisk. Start off slowly, before increasing the speed as the cream stiffens. Add the caster sugar and continue to whip until very stiff. Chill in the fridge.

6   Slice the banana and coat the pieces in the demerara sugar. Over a medium heat, fry the bananas on either side until browned. Serve the crumble with the whipped cream, melted caramel and fried bananas.

**TOP TIP ★** Make a separate half batch of crumble topping and bake on a small baking tray alongside the banoffee crumble for 15–20 minutes, then add to the top of the baked banoffee crumble. You can never have too much crumble topping!

# PEACH & PECAN CRUMBLE BARS

Here we've turned the traditional crumble into a lighter crumble bar, packed with lightly spiced peaches and finished with some vanilla buttercream and caramelized pecans. An easy picnic dessert.

## INGREDIENTS

*Makes 9*

### Crumble

600g (4⅔ cups) plain flour

1½ tsp baking powder

350g (1¾ cups packed) light soft brown sugar, plus 5–10g (1–2 tsp)

350g (3 sticks) unsalted butter

2 eggs

### Filling

750g (1lb 10oz) fresh peaches, peeled and stoned, or 3 x 410g (14½oz) cans of peaches, drained

75g (⅓ cup plus 1 tbsp packed) light soft brown sugar

125g (4½oz) pecans, chopped (optional)

1½ tsp ground sweet cinnamon

1 tsp ground nutmeg

10g (1 tbsp) cornflour, plus extra for the crumble

2 tbsp lemon juice

### Topping (optional)

50g (3½ tbsp) unsalted butter

100g (¾ cup) icing sugar

Vanilla extract, to taste

75ml (5 tbsp) water

75g (⅓ cup plus 1 tbsp packed) light soft brown sugar

1 tsp ground sweet cinnamon

50g (1¾oz) pecans

## SPECIAL EQUIPMENT

Food processor (optional)

23cm (9in) square tin or 20 x 30cm (8 x 12in) rectangular tin, lined

Piping bag and large nozzle

**1** Preheat the oven to 200°C (180°C fan/400°F/Gas 6).

**2** For the filling, chop the peaches into small chunks rather than slices. Mix the peaches with the sugar, pecans, if using, and the spices, then pour onto a baking tray. Bake for 15 minutes. Occasionally, open the oven and stir with a spoon.

**3** Next, make the crumble. This should be ready to bake alongside the peaches after they have been baking for 15 minutes. Place the flour, baking powder and sugar into a food processor and pulse until combined, or mix together by hand.

**4** Pulse or rub the butter into the flour until crumbs form, leaving some larger clumps. Add the eggs and slowly mix by hand, keeping it as crumbly as possible, but distributing the eggs evenly. Lightly press three-quarters of the crumble into the lined tin and pat down. Bake alongside the peaches for 15 minutes.

**5** Remove the peaches from the oven and drain off any excess liquid. Add the cornflour and mix together.

**6** Remove the crumble from the oven, sprinkle over a little cornflour, then evenly distribute the peaches over the top. Sprinkle over the remaining crumble and the 5–10g (1–2 tsp) light brown sugar and bake for a further 30 minutes until the crumble is golden brown. Leave to cool completely, then store in the fridge before slicing into squares, bars or triangles.

**7** If making the topping, beat together the butter and icing sugar. Add a drop or two of vanilla extract to flavour.

**8** In a pan, heat the water, light brown sugar and cinnamon over a medium heat, stirring constantly, for 1–2 minutes. Add the pecans and keep stirring while the syrup coats the nuts. Stir for 3 minutes. Pour the sugared pecans and syrup onto the lined baking tray and leave to cool. Break up once cold.

**9** Place the buttercream into a piping bag with a large piping nozzle fitted and pipe a few whips on top of each crumble bar. Decorate with the caramelized pecans.

# BLUEBERRY PIE CHEESECAKE BARS

Perfect for all seasons, these blueberry pie bars – complete with a helping of cheesecake – would be suitable to celebrate an autumnal get-together, a summer BBQ or our choice of event: an afternoon tea party. Forget Victoria sponge, scones or macarons – this dessert would fill you up after a few dainty sandwich triangles.

## INGREDIENTS

*Serves 9–12*

350g (2¾ cups) plain flour

1 tsp baking powder

250g (1 cup plus 4 tbsp packed) light soft brown sugar, plus 5–10g (1–2 tsp) for sprinkling

300g (2 sticks plus 4 tbsp) unsalted butter

2 eggs

### Filling

500g (1lb 2oz) blueberries

A dash of lemon juice

100g (½ cup) caster sugar

10g (1 tbsp) cornflour

### Cheesecake topping

65g (½ cup) icing sugar

1 tsp vanilla extract, or to taste

A dash of lemon juice

340g (11½oz) full-fat cream cheese

200ml (scant 1 cup) double cream

## SPECIAL EQUIPMENT

Food processor (optional)

23cm (9in) square tin or 20 x 30cm (8 x 12in) rectangular tin, lined

Baking tray

Mixer or hand-held electric whisk

Piping bag and large piping nozzle (optional)

1  Preheat the oven to 200°C (180°C fan/400°F/Gas 6).

2  For the filling, mix the blueberries with the lemon juice and caster sugar. Separate a small handful of the blueberries and place in the fridge – these will be used to make the blueberry compote. Add the cornflour to the remaining blueberries and make sure the berries are evenly coated.

3  To make the pie dough, place the flour, baking powder and sugar into a food processor and pulse until combined, or mix together by hand. Rub the butter into the flour until crumbs form, attempting to rid the butter of any larger lumps. Take a small handful of crumble and set aside – this will be used to sprinkle on top of the cheesecake later. Add the eggs and mix, then use your hands to form a dough.

4  Pat three-quarters of the dough into the lined tin and press down evenly. Pour the blueberries on top of the dough, before breaking up the remaining dough and placing pieces on top. It does not matter if there are lots of blueberries showing – the dough will spread during baking, leaving an attractive amount of blueberries showing. Sprinkle with the 5–10g (1–2 tsp) light brown sugar.

5  Bake for 35–40 minutes, or until the top is golden brown. Place the reserved crumble mixture onto a baking tray and bake alongside for 5–10 minutes, or until golden brown.

6  Leave the blueberry pie bar in the tin to cool completely, then chill in the fridge before slicing into rectangles, squares or triangles. ▶

### Cheesecake and topping

*7*    Whisk together the icing sugar, vanilla extract, lemon juice and cream cheese for a minute or so until smooth and slightly thickened.

*8*    In a separate bowl, whip the double cream until thick. Fold the thickened cream through the cream cheese mixture until combined. Chill in the fridge overnight (or for at least 5–6 hours).

*9*    Retrieve the reserved blueberries and place them either in a pan or a heatproof bowl. Add 20ml (4 tsp) of water and heat gently over a low heat or in the microwave for 30–40 seconds at a time. Stir and heat until the blueberries have started to burst and you have a deep purple compote. Leave to cool.

*10*    Use a palette knife to swirl some cheesecake mixture on top of each bar, or load the cheesecake mixture into a piping bag fitted with a large piping nozzle and pipe a large whip on top of each blueberry square. Spoon some cold blueberry compote on top and sprinkle over some reserved crumble to decorate.

**TOP TIPS**

★ Using fruit can compromise the bake, so it is best to eat the crumble bar on the day it is made or the following day.

★ The cheesecake topping is interchangeable with ganache too, so if you would like to swap to either of these we have fabulous recipes on page 201.

# UNICORN CRÈME BRÛLÉE

This creamy custard dessert is surprisingly easy to make and we have added a fun and colourful twist on the classic recipe to impress your guests (whether they're adults or children). Kids and grown-ups alike will enjoy cracking through the unicorn-inspired hard sugar exterior to find a delightful pink strawberry custard underneath. If you'd prefer the original, use vanilla extract or a vanilla pod for a rich and decadent French favourite.

## INGREDIENTS

*Makes 4*

**Custard**

5 egg yolks

75g (6 tbsp) golden caster sugar

500ml (generous 2 cups) double cream

Pink food colouring (oil-based is best)

Strawberry flavouring (we used Foodie Flavours), to taste

**Topping**

8 tsp golden caster sugar

Food colourings (we used oil-based baby blue and pink)

## SPECIAL EQUIPMENT

Mixer or hand-held electric whisk

4 x 9cm (3½in) ramekins

Deep baking tray

Kitchen blowtorch (optional)

1   Preheat the oven to 180°C (160°C fan/350°F/Gas 4).

2   Put the egg yolks into a heatproof bowl and add the sugar. Use a mixer or a hand-held electric whisk to cream the yolks and sugar together until the yolks appear stiff and pale.

3   Pour the double cream into a saucepan and heat gently. Add some oil-based pink food colouring to the cream until it reaches your desired shade and mix until well incorporated with no streaks.

4   Add some drops of flavouring – we used around 20 drops, however, depending on the brand, you may need more or less. Mix well. Heat for 5–10 minutes over a low heat until small bubbles appear around the side – do not let the cream get too hot or the mixture may turn into scrambled eggs.

5   Once the bubbles appear, take the cream off the heat and slowly pour into the egg yolk and sugar mixture while whisking. Strain the mixture through a sieve to catch any larger lumps and then use a spoon to scoop the foam off the top of the liquid (there may be a lot of it). This will ensure a really smooth creamy custard.

6   Once the liquid is free from lumps and foam, divide the mixture between the four ramekins. Place the ramekins in the deep baking tray or in an ovenproof dish that comes higher than the ramekins – a cake tin would also do!

7   Boil the kettle, then place the baking tray in the oven. Pour the boiling water into the baking tray so that it reaches halfway up the ramekins (this will enable no spilling while walking over to the oven!). Loosely cover the baking tray with foil, ensuring there is a small gap for air to escape, and bake for 45 minutes, or until there is a slight jiggle in the middle of the custard. ▶

**8**  Remove the baking tray from the oven, leave to cool slightly and remove the ramekins from the boiling water. Set aside and once fully cooled, refrigerate for at least 3 hours or overnight.

**9**  Evenly split the sugar for the topping into how many colours you'd like to use on the top. Using oil-based colouring, place a few drops of the desired colours into the sugar and mix with a spoon or a clean finger (we feel fingers work best!). We have used baby blue and pink, and then mixed them together to make a purple.

**10**  Sprinkle about 2 teaspoons of sugar over each custard, making sure to use some of each colour and slightly overlap them.

**11**  Use a kitchen blowtorch to caramelize the sugar so that the colours start to melt and blend together, and some golden spots start to appear. (See also Tip below.)

**12**  Once all of the sugar crusts have been caramelized, serve immediately or within 20–30 minutes.

**TOP TIP** ★ You can also use a preheated hot grill to caramelize the sugar, however, you will not have as much control as with a kitchen blowtorch. Make sure to keep your eyes on the grill as the sugar can easily burn.

# SUMMER FRUITS MINI PIES

Dainty pies served cold for a summer afternoon tea or warm with a hot brew in the winter months, these mince pie-sized treats are super cute and fun to make.

## INGREDIENTS

*Makes 12*

300g (2½ cups) plain flour

30g (2½ tbsp) granulated sugar, plus extra for sprinkling

½ tsp salt

250g (2 sticks) cold unsalted butter

8 tbsp ice-cold water

1 egg

2 tbsp milk

### Filling

150g (5½oz) frozen mixed summer fruits

60g (5 tbsp) caster sugar

½ tsp ground sweet cinnamon

2 heaped tbsp cornflour

## SPECIAL EQUIPMENT

Food processor (optional)

10cm (4in) cookie cutter

12-hole cupcake tin, greased with cake release spray

Lattice pastry cutter

Pastry brush

**TOP TIP ★** The lattice and cookie cutters are optional. For the topping, you can use a knife to cut strips of the pastry and layer in a criss-cross pattern, pushing the pastry into the sides to join together. If you don't have cookie cutters, use a sharp knife to cut a circle to match the size of the cupcake tin.

*1* If making the dough by hand, add the dry ingredients to a bowl. Grate in the butter (or add as small cubes) and use your hands to coat the butter with the dry mixture. Sift and rub the butter through your fingers until crumbs form. Add the water and mix with a spoon until a dough forms. If using a food processor, pulse the flour, sugar and salt together. Cut the butter into cubes, add to the flour, then pulse until breadcrumbs form. Add the water and mix until a dough forms.

*2* Remove the dough and pat down with some flour if too sticky. Wrap in cling film and chill for 1–2 hours, or longer if possible.

*3* Roll out the pastry until 2–3mm (1⁄16–1⁄8in) thick and stamp out 12 circles with the cookie cutter. From the centre, slice a line to the edge of each circle. Press a pastry circle into each cupcake hole using the cut to help curve around the hole, then press the cut edges together to seal. Chill the tin and the remaining pastry.

*4* To prepare the filling, weigh out most of the mixed frozen fruit (save some large pieces of fruit), place into a saucepan and combine with the sugar, cinnamon and a splash of water. As the fruit softens, cut any large fruit in half. Simmer for 10 minutes, then add the cornflour and mix until coated. Leave to cool.

*5* Spoon equal amounts of the cooled fruit into the cupcake cases, and then add the larger frozen pieces. This will enable the pies to be filled but stop the filling bubbling up out of them.

*6* Roll out the remaining pastry to 2–3mm (1⁄16–1⁄8in) thick and use the lattice cutter to create the perfect pastry pattern – or cut strips of pastry using a sharp knife and weave them over each pie in an under and over formation, pressing the edges together to seal. Chill again for a further 30 minutes – the pastry needs to be cold before baking.

*7* Preheat the oven to 200°C (180°C fan/400°F/Gas 6). Whisk the egg and milk together. Brush over the lids and sprinkle with sugar. Bake for 25 minutes until the filling is bubbling and the pastry is golden. Leave in the tin until slightly cooled. Serve with any leftover fruit, cream, ice cream or custard!

# APPLE & BLACKBERRY PIE PARCELS

Hand-held-sized, flaky pie-crust pastry parcels brimming with a stewed spiced apple and blackberry filling, sprinkled with sugar for the crunch. This recipe will make six simple rectangular parcels or four of the more complex plaited lattice designs. Autumnal baking at its most delicious. Enjoy on a crisp morning walk with your pals, fresh out of the oven.

## INGREDIENTS

*Makes 4 or 6*

### Pastry

300g (2½ cups) plain flour

30g (2½ tbsp) granulated sugar

½ tsp salt

250g (2 sticks) cold unsalted butter

8 tbsp ice-cold water

### Filling

200ml (scant 1 cup) water

1 tbsp lemon juice

200g (1 cup packed) light soft brown sugar

400g (14oz) cooking apples, peeled, cored and chopped into small pieces

100g (3½oz) blackberries

1 tsp ground sweet cinnamon

1 tsp cornflour (optional)

### Egg wash

1 egg

2 tbsp milk

### Topping

25g (2 tbsp) granulated sugar

25g (2 tbsp) light soft brown sugar

A sprinkling of icing sugar (optional)

## SPECIAL EQUIPMENT

Food processor (optional)

Mixer (optional)

Baking tray(s), lined

Pastry brush

## Pastry

1   As the pastry needs to be chilled, it can be made in advance. If making by hand (our preferred method), add the dry ingredients to a bowl. Grate in the butter (or add as small cubes) and use your hands to coat the butter with the dry mixture. Sift and rub the butter through your fingers until crumbs form. Add the water and mix with a spoon until a dough forms. If using a food processor, pulse the flour, sugar and salt together. Cut the butter into cubes, add to the flour, then pulse until breadcrumbs form. Add the water and mix until a dough forms.

2   Remove the dough and pat down with some flour if too sticky. Wrap in cling film and chill for 1–2 hours, or longer if possible.

## Filling

3   Put the water, lemon juice and sugar into a saucepan over a medium heat and mix. Add the apples and allow the water to start to boil. Add the blackberries and cinnamon and turn down the heat. Allow to bubble for about 5 minutes, or until the juices become slightly thickened. If too wet, add 1 teaspoon of cornflour; if too dry, add some more water.

## To make the pie parcels

4   Roll out the pastry using a rolling pin to around 5mm (¼in) thick. Use a pizza cutter or knife to cut out 4–12 equal-sized rectangles, about 7.5 x 10cm (3 x 4in). The number will depend on the type of parcels you are making – for a closed pie, you will need two rectangles per pie; if you are making a lattice pie, you will need one rectangle per pie. ▶

**5**   Lay four or six pastry rectangles on the lined baking tray(s). Spoon 1 heaped tablespoon of filling into the centre of each rectangle. Whisk the egg and milk together to make an egg wash. Brush some egg wash around the perimeter of each pastry rectangle using a pastry brush.

**6**   If you are making the six rectangular parcels, cut some slits or make some holes in the top of the remaining rectangles to release steam while baking, and then stick the two pastry rectangles together. Pinch down using your fingers.

**7**   If you are making the four plaited lattice crusts, cut out long strips of pastry and position them in overlapping strips over the filling. Tightly plait three pieces together for more decoration, draping the plait over each rectangle in different directions, making sure that the edges of the pies are being covered. Plaiting pastry uses up a lot of it! Make sure to keep all the pastry in the fridge while not in use to keep it cold.

**8**   Use fork prongs or a knife to make small slits around all the edges of each parcel or cut off any excess pastry from the strips and plaits that may be hanging over the edge of the pie parcels.

**9**   Chill in the freezer for 20 minutes to ensure the pastry is still cold and preheat the oven to 200°C (180°C fan/400°F/Gas 6). Make the sugar topping by mixing the granulated sugar and light brown sugar together in a bowl.

**10**   Brush the pie parcels with more egg wash and sprinkle with the sugar topping, making sure all the tops are covered. Bake for 25 minutes, or until golden brown. Remove from the oven and eat warm or cold. Sift some icing sugar over the top to finish, if you like.

**TOP TIPS**

★ Handling the pastry so much during the plaiting process will allow the butter to start melting. Make sure the pastry is in the fridge while not in use as the colder the pastry is before it goes into the oven, the better chance it has at holding its shape during baking, which is imperative with the decorative plaits.

★ Depending on which shaped parcels you choose to make, there may be some fruit filling left over. Enjoy on the side, use in another recipe or freeze for up to 3 months and use again.

# INDIVIDUAL NUTELLA TRIFLES

The traditional trifle adorns many tables during festivities but too often with soggy sponge fingers and too much sherry! This decadent chocolate version will impress everyone around the dinner table.

## INGREDIENTS

*Makes 6*

420g (15oz) chocolate brownies, plus extra (optional) to decorate

### Chocolate sponge

100g (½ cup) golden caster sugar

1 egg

60g (4 tbsp) unsalted butter

40g (¼ cup) plain flour

½ tsp salt

½ tsp baking powder

25g (¼ cup) cocoa powder

¼ tsp espresso powder

25ml (5 tsp) vegetable oil

### Chocolate custard

500ml (generous 2 cups) custard

100g (⅓ cup plus 2 tbsp) Nutella

50g (1¾oz) dark chocolate

### Nutella whipped cream

600ml (2½ cups) double cream

3 tbsp icing sugar

75g (⅓ cup) Nutella

### Decoration (optional)

100g (⅓ cup plus 2 tbsp) Nutella

Hazelnut nibs

Hazelnut chocolate wafers

Nutella biscuits

Ferrero Rocher, halved

Kinder bar, broken into pieces

## SPECIAL EQUIPMENT

Mixer or hand-held electric whisk

900g (2lb) loaf tin, lined

Piping bags and large open star nozzle

Serving or individual trifle glasses

1   Cut the brownies – 70g (2½oz) per trifle – into small chunks to use later.

2   To make the chocolate sponge, preheat the oven to 180°C (160°C fan/350°F/Gas 4).

3   Whisk together the sugar and egg for a couple of minutes until pale and thick. Gently melt the butter in a saucepan on the hob or in short bursts in the microwave. Sift the flour, salt, baking powder and cocoa powder together into a bowl before folding into the egg and sugar.

4   Pour a dash of boiling water into the espresso powder and leave to dissolve. Add this, the vegetable oil and the melted butter to the batter and stir until smooth. Pour into the lined loaf tin and bake for about 22 minutes, or until the sponge springs back when pressed. Leave to cool.

5   To make the chocolate custard, pour the custard into a saucepan over a low heat, then add the Nutella and break in the dark chocolate. Gently mix together until melted and combined. Remove from the heat, leave to cool and then place in the fridge until required.

6   If you want to use Nutella to decorate, gently heat the Nutella in the microwave until runny and load into a piping bag. Snip off the very end so only a small amount of sauce comes out at once. This can be piped in small quantities between each layer to accentuate the Nutella taste!

7   If using, pipe some Nutella into the bottom of the serving/trifle glasses, to taste. Place 70g (2½oz) of the cubed brownies into the bottom of each glass and use your fingers to gently press them down to ensure the custard will not drip through the cracks too much (we want even layers!). ▶

**8** Drizzle some more Nutella on top of the brownies, if using. Spoon around 100g (3½oz) of the cold chocolate custard onto the brownie layer, using the back of a spoon to evenly coat and allow the custard to be visible on the outside of the glass.

**9** Drizzle over some more Nutella, if using. Crumble the cooled chocolate sponge on top of the custard, again taking the layer up to the edge of the glass to ensure the third layer is visible. We then drizzled some more Nutella on top of the sponge, so do so now if you like.

**10** Whip the double cream on a low to medium speed, waiting until soft to stiff peaks have formed. Add the icing sugar, 1 tablespoon at a time, and then the Nutella, still whisking until fully incorporated. Load the Nutella whipped cream into a piping bag fitted with a large open star nozzle and pipe on top of each trifle.

**11** Finish by decorating to your taste – we used hazelnut nibs, hazelnut wafers, Nutella biscuits, more brownie cubes, Ferrero Rocher and piece of Kinder bar!

**TOP TIP** ★ Like a lot of our recipes, this trifle is really versatile, so change up the flavours if you want. Try omitting the Nutella, or adding in different flavours such as Biscoff or chocolate orange.

# BISCOFF PANNA COTTA

Panna cotta is much simpler to make than you think – this creamy Italian dessert uses gelatine to thicken so isn't a custard, and not quite a flan, but melts in your mouth like a milky jelly. We've added Biscoff for richness and flavour and it is absolutely delicious! So pull out your ramekins for the next dinner party. Try adding Nutella instead of Biscoff spread for a chocolate hazelnut version!

## INGREDIENTS

*Makes 4*

150ml (⅔ cup) full-fat milk

12g (¼oz) powdered gelatine or 4 leaves of gelatine

100g (⅓ cup plus 2 tbsp) Lotus Biscoff spread

350ml (1½ cups) double cream

50g (¼ cup) caster sugar

Vanilla extract, to taste

**Topping**

Squirty cream (optional)

Lotus Biscoff spread, melted

Lotus Biscoff biscuits, crushed or left whole

## SPECIAL EQUIPMENT

4 coupe glasses or 9cm (3½in) ramekins

1   Pour 50ml (3½ tbsp) of the milk into a bowl. Add the powdered gelatine or the gelatine leaves and set aside for 5 minutes or so.

2   Heat the Biscoff spread in short bursts in the microwave until runny. Add the melted spread to a saucepan along with the cream, the remaining 100ml (6½ tbsp) of milk and the sugar. Heat very gently and mix until all the ingredients are incorporated – do not bring to a simmer or boil.

3   Pour in the gelatine and milk once the gelatine has bloomed (powder) or become soft (leaves). Continue to heat gently and stir until all the gelatine has dissolved.

4   Once incorporated, remove from the heat before straining through a sieve to catch any lumps.

5   Stir in the vanilla extract to taste and leave to cool for a few minutes. Split between the serving glasses or ramekins and leave to cool completely before setting in the fridge for a minimum of 6 hours (or overnight).

6   Once set, store in the fridge until you are ready to serve and decorate to your taste. Decorate with squirty cream, if using, then drizzle with melted Biscoff spread and sprinkle with crushed biscuits or add a whole biscuit to each portion. You could even try coating the rim of each glass with melted Biscoff spread and then dipping it into Biscoff crumbs. The ramekins can also be flipped upside down to remove the panna cotta to serve, if desired.

# SALTED CARAMEL GANACHE POTS

This rich dessert should chill for several hours before serving, which is just as well as it would sometimes take me locking it in the fridge to stop me spooning it hot out of the pot! There's no wastage in this recipe for two, served up in glasses to admire the contrasting layers, simply decorated with sea salt and strawberries. Romantic date night completed. As this dessert is extremely decadent, it can also be split between four small serving glasses.

## INGREDIENTS

*Makes 2 or 4*

**Salted caramel**

150g (⅔ cup) granulated sugar

60ml (4 tbsp) water

50g (3½ tbsp) unsalted butter

125ml (½ cup) double cream

1 tsp vanilla extract

Sea salt, to taste

**Milk chocolate ganache**

60ml (4 tbsp) double cream

120g (4¼oz) milk chocolate

**Decoration**

Sea salt

Fruit, such as strawberries

## SPECIAL EQUIPMENT

2 or 4 (small) glasses or dessert pots

1   Place the sugar and water in a saucepan, stir and set over a low-medium heat. Allow the sugar to dissolve before turning up the heat slightly. The caramel will start turning a darker amber colour, do not stir but allow it to bubble for 6–7 minutes. While making caramel before, I have ended up with what looked like wet sand at the bottom of my pan after starting to boil the water. If this happens, increase the heat as the water has all evaporated but the sugar syrup has not caramelized!

2   Remove from the heat and add the butter and cream, this may bubble. Return to the heat and continue to whisk quickly for another 3–4 minutes. Remove from the heat and stir in the vanilla extract and some sea salt to taste.

3   Immediately pour the caramel into the serving glasses, or if these are not heatproof, pour the caramel into another bowl to cool so the saucepan does not continue to cook the caramel. Once slightly cooler, pour the caramel into the bottom half of the serving glasses. Leave to cool and then place in the fridge.

4   To make the ganache, heat the cream and chocolate gently over a bain-marie or in short bursts in the microwave. Stir until incorporated, thick and glossy and then split the ganache between the serving glasses. Leave to cool and then set in the fridge. Sprinkle some sea salt on top to taste and decorate each glass with a strawberry or two. Remove from the fridge a few hours before serving, this will enable the ganache and caramel to be soft enough to dig into with a spoon.

**Note**

Cooking with hot/melted sugar can be extremely dangerous. Please wear protection if required!

# TRAY BAKES & LOAF CAKES

# RED VELVET CHEESECAKE BLONDIES

These fudgy red velvet blondies are halfway between a blondie and brownie as the recipe uses white chocolate, vanilla extract and cocoa powder. The perfectly blended flavours of chocolate, vanilla and tangy cheesecake make each mouthful a dream to eat – just don't use too much red food colouring or you'll end up with a stained mouth!

## INGREDIENTS

*Makes 8–10*

100g (½ cup) caster sugar

100g (½ cup packed) light soft brown sugar

2 eggs plus 1 egg yolk

100g (3½oz) white chocolate

170g (1½ sticks) unsalted butter

30g (1½ tbsp) golden syrup

1 tsp vanilla extract

Red gel food colouring (use whatever shade of red you'd like)

50g (½ cup) cocoa power

200g (scant 1½ cups) plain flour

1 tbsp cornflour

150g (5½oz) white chocolate chunks (optional)

**Cheesecake topping**

350g (12oz) full-fat cream cheese

50g (¼ cup) caster sugar

50g (¼ cup) golden caster sugar

1 egg plus 1 egg yolk

3 tbsp lemon juice

20g (1 tbsp plus 1 tsp) plain flour

## SPECIAL EQUIPMENT

Mixer or hand-held electric whisk

23cm (9in) square tin or 20 x 30cm (8 x 12in) rectangular tin, lined

1 Leave all the ingredients to come to room temperature for 1 hour before making the cheesecake mixture first. Preheat the oven to 175°C (155°C fan/345°F/Gas 3½).

2 Whisk the cream cheese in a mixer for 2–3 minutes until creamy (or in a mixing bowl with a hand-held electric whisk). Slowly pour in both sugars and mix until incorporated.

3 Lightly beat the egg and egg yolk separately, then add to the cream cheese mixture. Do not overbeat the egg as this can incorporate air bubbles into the cheesecake, causing it to crack. Finish by adding the lemon juice and folding in the flour with a spatula. Scrape the sides of the bowl and mix to make sure any lumps have been mixed in, however, do not overmix as this can also cause the cheesecake to crack. Place the cheesecake mixture in the fridge until needed.

4 Whisk both sugars, the eggs and egg yolk in a bowl with a hand-held electric whisk or in a mixer.

5 In another bowl or pan, break up the white chocolate and add the butter. Melt gently together in the microwave using short bursts of 10–20 seconds or over a bain-marie. Stir until combined and the mixture is smooth.

6 Slowly pour the melted chocolate mixture and golden syrup into the bowl with the whisked eggs and sugar. Add the vanilla extract and the red food colouring and mix until combined. Finally, sift in the cocoa powder, flour and cornflour and hand mix, making sure to scrape around the sides of the bowl and incorporate all of the dry ingredients. Add the chocolate chunks, if using, and mix until evenly distributed throughout the batter.

7 Pour all but a spoonful or two of the blondie batter into the lined tin. Leave this to sit for 5 minutes to enable the batter to slightly firm up – this will allow the cheesecake mixture to sit on top of it rather than sink into it. ▶

**8** Pour the cheesecake mixture over the top of the blondie batter and use the back of a spoon to evenly distribute it. Whisk 1 tablespoon of boiling water at a time into the remaining blondie batter to thin the consistency to match that of the cheesecake. Spoon on top of the cheesecake layer in small blobs or lines and use a knife to either feather or swirl the mixture in. You can even drizzle it on top in patterns – it depends on how you'd like the final result to look!

**9** Bake for 45 minutes. The blondie should slightly jiggle once it is out of the oven. Leave to cool completely in the tin, then transfer to the fridge. A tip for fudgy brownies is to not just refrigerate them for a few hours but let them chill overnight.

**10** To serve, use a hot knife and make sure to wipe the knife in between each slice to ensure a clean cut. Or you can use small, shaped cookie cutters to cut out different shapes, such as circles or hearts.

**TOP TIPS** ★ We use Sugarflair Red Extra food colouring paste in these blondies and we find you don't need much to turn them a deep red colour. The more you use, the brighter the shade will be, however, this can compromise the texture and the taste of the blondie, so don't use too much. If the quality of the red food colouring isn't very good, add the cocoa powder last, using a small amount at a time to ensure the mixture is the right colour. ★ We also recommend using bake-stable chocolate chips to prevent them from melting in the blondies.

# CHEESECAKE BROWNIES

After a recent trip to New York, we were inspired to put together a simple cheesecake recipe to top a variation of our signature brownie – rich yet creamy, with a subtle hint of tanginess.

## INGREDIENTS

*Makes 8–10*

3 eggs

150g (5½oz) dark chocolate

270g (2 sticks plus 2 tbsp) unsalted butter

270g (1⅓ cups) golden caster sugar

100g (1 cup) cocoa powder

120g (scant 1 cup) plain flour

½ tsp fine instant coffee

**Cheesecake topping**

350g (12oz) full-fat cream cheese

50g (¼ cup) caster sugar

50g (¼ cup) golden caster sugar

1 egg plus 1 egg yolk

Dash of lemon juice

20g (1 tbsp plus 1 tsp) plain flour

## SPECIAL EQUIPMENT

Hand-held electric whisk or mixer

23cm (9in) square tin or 20 x 30cm (8 x 12in) rectangular tin, lined

*1* Leave all the ingredients out for 1 hour to come to room temperature. Preheat the oven to 180°C (160°C fan/350°F/Gas 4).

*2* For the cheesecake topping, whisk the cream cheese in a mixer for 2–3 minutes until creamy (or in a mixing bowl with a hand-held electric whisk). Pour in both sugars and mix until combined.

*3* Lightly beat the egg and egg yolk separately and add to the mixture. Add the lemon juice and fold in the flour with a spatula. Do not overmix, as this can cause the cheesecake to crack. Chill in the fridge until needed.

*4* Whisk the eggs with a hand-held electric whisk or in a mixer. Gently heat the chocolate and butter together over a low heat on the hob, or in short bursts in the microwave. Stir until smooth.

*5* Slowly pour the melted chocolate mixture into the eggs and add the sugar. Mix until combined. Sift in the cocoa powder and flour. Cover the coffee in enough boiling water to dissolve, and mix it in.

*6* Pour all but a spoonful or two of the brownie batter into the lined tin. Leave this to sit for 5 minutes to enable the batter to slightly firm up – this will allow the cheesecake mixture to sit on top of it rather than sink into it.

*7* Pour the cheesecake topping over the top of the brownie and use the back of a spoon to evenly distribute it. Whisk a small amount of boiling water into the remaining brownie batter to thin the consistency to match that of the cheesecake topping. Spoon small blobs or lines over the brownie and use a knife to feather or swirl the mixture in. You can even drizzle the mixture on top in patterns – it depends on how you'd like the final result!

*8* Bake for 40 minutes. The brownie should slightly jiggle once it is out of the oven. Leave to cool completely in the tin, then transfer to the fridge.

*9* Slice into whatever sized brownie you'd like! These are extremely rich, so we recommend cutting into small pieces.

# CHERRY BAKEWELL BLONDIES

Blondies are definitely one of our bestsellers and our Cherry Bakewell ones are a personal favourite! Fudgy pieces of white chocolate and almond, swirled with cherry jam and filled with glacé cherries; every bite is a Bakewell lover's dream!

## INGREDIENTS

*Makes 8–10*

220g (2 sticks) unsalted butter

125g (4½oz) white chocolate

3 eggs

125g (⅔ cup) caster sugar

125g (½ cup plus 2 tbsp) light soft brown sugar

40g (2 tbsp) golden syrup

Pink gel food colouring (optional)

5–10 drops of almond extract, to taste

285g (2 cups plus 2 tbsp) plain flour

1 heaped tsp cornflour

¼ tsp salt

200g (7oz) white chocolate chips

150g (5½oz) glacé cherries

180g (6oz) cherry jam or conserve

## SPECIAL EQUIPMENT

Mixer or hand-held electric whisk

20 x 30cm (8 x 12in) tin, lined

Piping bag

1   Preheat the oven to 200°C (180°C fan/400°F/Gas 6).

2   Using a microwave, or over a bain-marie, melt the butter and white chocolate together.

3   Combine the eggs, both sugars, the golden syrup and a little pink food colouring, if using, in a mixer. Add the melted chocolate mixture. Scrape the mixture around the sides and bottom with a spatula before mixing again.

4   Pour in the almond extract, to taste. Sift the flour and cornflour together and pour into the wet mixture. Add the salt and 150g (5½oz) of the chocolate chips, mixing on a low-speed setting and remembering to scrape down the sides with a spatula to make sure all the ingredients combine.

5   Fold in 100g (3½oz) of the glacé cherries with a spatula. Pour the batter into the lined tin and load a piping bag with the cherry jam. Snip off the tip of the piping bag and pipe lines of jam into the batter. Use a skewer to drag the jam in circles, making sure it is evenly spread. Scatter over the remaining white chocolate chips and press in the remaining cherries.

6   Bake for 35 minutes. It may look under-baked and the middle should still wobble when it comes out of the oven. Leave to cool completely in the tin, then chill in the fridge for at least 6 hours or overnight before cutting into squares or rectangles to serve.

> **TOP TIP ★** Use bake-stable white chocolate chips in the blondie mixture to ensure they don't melt while baking.

# CHURRO BLONDIES WITH DULCE DE LECHE DIPPING SAUCE

Churros may have originated in Spain and Portugal, but we've enjoyed them homemade after a Mexican fiesta with our friends on a themed evening. This blondie version may not require deep-frying, but the crunch from the churro combined with the sweetest of the dulce de leche is (almost) as good.

## INGREDIENTS

Makes 20

220g (2 sticks) unsalted butter

125g (4½oz) white chocolate

3 eggs

250g (1 cup plus 4 tbsp) light soft brown sugar

40g (2 tbsp) golden syrup

1 heaped tsp ground sweet cinnamon

285g (2 cups plus 2 tbsp) plain flour

100g (3½oz) milk chocolate chips

### Topping

30g (2½ tbsp) light soft brown sugar

30g (2½ tbsp) granulated sugar

¼ tsp salt

1 tsp ground sweet cinnamon

### Dulce de leche

397g (14oz) can of condensed milk

OR

1 litre (4 cups plus 3 tbsp) full-fat milk

300g (1½ cups packed) light soft brown sugar

2 tsp vanilla extract

Pinch of bicarbonate of soda

## SPECIAL EQUIPMENT

Mixer or hand-held electric whisk

23cm (9in) square tin or 20 x 30cm (8 x 12in) rectangular tin, lined

Piping bag

### Dulce de leche

There are easy ways to make dulce de leche – one which is more simple and less restrictive than the other.

The easy method is to place the can of condensed milk in a pan. Submerge the can in water, making sure the water level is above the can. Bring the water to the boil and, once it is bubbling, reduce the heat and simmer for 3 hours, making sure the can is always covered with water. Leave to cool in the water and then open when necessary. The dulce de leche can be refrigerated in the unopened can for up to a month.

If you'd like to make dulce de leche from scratch, you will need to continuously check and stir the mixture. Heat the milk in a saucepan over a medium heat, then add the sugar and vanilla extract. Stir well. Turn up the heat to medium-high and, once the milk has started to boil and bubble, add the bicarbonate of soda. This may start to bubble but will soon settle. Turn down the heat.

Stir every 5–10 minutes for 1½ hours, making sure the sauce is not burning. Once it becomes thick and caramel-like in consistency, stir continuously for 10–15 minutes. The liquid should have reduced to a much smaller quantity. Take off the heat and leave to cool before using.

Store in the fridge for up to 7 days.

### Churro blondies

1  Preheat the oven to 160°C (140°C fan/325°F/Gas 3).

2  Gently heat the butter and white chocolate in a pan on the hob or in the microwave in short bursts until the butter and chocolate have fully melted. Mix until combined. ▶

**3**   In a mixer, whisk together the eggs and sugar. Add the melted chocolate mixture and golden syrup and mix until incorporated.

**4**   Add the cinnamon and flour and fold together using a spatula, or on the lowest setting of the mixer. Stir in the chocolate chips.

**5**   In a separate bowl, make the topping. Mix both sugars, the salt and cinnamon together using a spoon. Pour half of the cinnamon sugar into the lined tin and spread evenly. Next, pour the blondie batter on top, using the back of a spoon to gently spread the batter on top of the cinnamon sugar, taking care not to disrupt the positioning of the sugar.

**6**   Place around half of the dulce de leche into a piping bag, snip off the tip and pipe neat lines along the tin. Using a sharp knife or a skewer, feather the dulce de leche into the blondie mixture. Sprinkle the remaining cinnamon sugar over the top of the blondie. Bake for 25–30 minutes, or until there is a small jiggle when the blondie is moved.

**7**   Leave to cool in the tin, then chill in the fridge overnight to set. Once cold, slice into finger-shaped rectangles and serve with the remaining dulce de leche sauce to dip into.

**TOP TIPS ★** Using the condensed milk method to make dulce de leche is less time restrictive as you do not constantly have to be stirring the mixture. Dulce de leche can also be made in advance and stored in the fridge if you would like to prepare it before making these blondies. ★ We advise using bake-stable chocolate chips in the blondie mixture so that they don't melt in the oven.

# CORNFLAKE BLONDIES

If you want a trip down memory lane to your primary school pudding, these cornflake tart blondies will take you there. Our original blondie recipe swirled with raspberry jam and topped with chewy cornflakes is a number one seller at our bakery, served either alone or with hot custard. Use bake-stable chocolate chips that stay solid in the blondie mixture.

## INGREDIENTS

*Makes 8–10*

220g (2 sticks) unsalted butter

125g (4½oz) white chocolate

3 eggs

125g (½ cup plus 2 tbsp) light soft brown sugar

125g (⅔ cup) caster sugar

285g (2 cups plus 2 tbsp) plain flour

¼ tsp salt

1 heaped tsp cornflour

5 drops of vanilla extract

40g (2 tbsp) golden syrup

200g (7oz) white chocolate chips

180g (6oz) raspberry jam

### Cornflake topping

50g (3½ tbsp) unsalted butter

125g (½ cup) golden syrup

25g (2 tbsp) light soft brown sugar

120g (4¼oz) cornflakes

## SPECIAL EQUIPMENT

Mixer or hand-held electric whisk

23cm (9in) square tin or 20 x 30cm (8 x 12in) rectangular tin, lined

1   Preheat the oven to 160°C (140°C fan/325°F/Gas 3).

2   Using a microwave, or a pan on the hob, melt the butter with the white chocolate.

3   In a mixer, whisk together the eggs and both sugars until combined. Once melted, add the butter and chocolate mixture and continue mixing. Remember to scrape the mixture around the sides and bottom of the bowl with a spatula.

4   Sift the flour, salt and cornflour together and add to the mixture with the vanilla extract and golden syrup. When it has combined, add 150g (5½oz) of the white chocolate chips and stir with a spatula (using the mixer may start melting the chips), scraping down the sides to mix thoroughly.

5   Pour the blondie batter into the lined tin, making sure it is evenly spread. Melt the jam in the microwave, or in a pan on the hob, and spoon splodges over the top of the batter. Use a skewer to swirl the jam through the mixture, right up to the edges. Scatter the remaining 50g (1¾oz) of chocolate chips over the top.

6   Bake for 23 minutes – the middle should still wobble when it is removed from the oven.

7   While the blondie is baking, prepare the cornflake topping. Melt together the butter, golden syrup and sugar. Measure out the cornflakes into a large bowl and pour the liquid over the top. Use a spoon to mix together, ensuring all of the cornflakes are completely coated.

8   Carefully spoon the cornflake topping over the blondie in an even layer. Bake for a further 12 minutes – it should still have a slight wobble. Leave to cool completely in the tin, then chill in the fridge for at least 6 hours (preferably overnight).

9   Cut up and enjoy! Usually custard goes well with cornflake tart, but these are just as fabulous on their own.

# CINNAMON ROLL BLONDIES

Our white chocolate blondie but with the taste of autumn, winter and Christmas rolled into one. Swirled with cinnamon roll filling and cream cheese, it begs the question – could cinnamon roll filling be the new pumpkin spice? Use bake-stable chocolate chips in the blondie to keep their shape during baking.

## INGREDIENTS

*Makes 8–10*

**Blondie**

220g (2 sticks) unsalted butter

125g (4½oz) white chocolate

3 eggs

125g (½ cup plus 2 tbsp) light soft brown sugar

125g (⅔ cup) caster sugar

40g (2 tbsp) golden syrup

2 tsp ground sweet cinnamon

¼ tsp salt

1 heaped tsp cornflour

285g (2 cups plus 2 tbsp) plain flour

150g (5½oz) white chocolate chips

100g (⅔ cup) sultanas (optional)

**Cream cheese filling**

45g (1½oz) full-fat cream cheese

50g (⅓ cup) icing sugar, plus extra if needed

A dash of lemon juice

2 tsp cornflour

**Filling**

25g (1½ tbsp) unsalted butter

40g (3¼ tbsp) dark soft brown sugar

1 tsp ground sweet cinnamon

## SPECIAL EQUIPMENT

Mixer or hand-held electric whisk

23cm (9in) square tin or 20 x 30cm (8 x 12in) rectangular tin, lined

Piping bags

*1* Prepare the cream cheese filling. Using the whisk attachment on a mixer, whip the cream cheese. Add the icing sugar (no need to sift), lemon juice and cornflour. If needed, add an extra 1 teaspoon of icing sugar at a time until it is the consistency of royal icing. Place in the freezer for later – this is best used after it has been frozen for several hours.

*2* Preheat the oven to 160°C (140°C fan/325°F/Gas 3).

*3* To make the filling, mix together the butter, sugar and cinnamon. Set aside.

*4* Using a microwave, or a bain-marie, melt the butter with the white chocolate.

*5* In a mixer, combine the eggs and both sugars. Add the melted chocolate mixture and golden syrup and continue mixing. Remember to scrape the mixture around the sides and bottom of the bowl with a spatula.

*6* Add the cinnamon, salt, cornflour and flour and mix until combined. Then, with a spatula, fold in the white chocolate chips and sultanas, if using, scraping down the sides to thoroughly mix (using a mixer may start melting the chips).

*7* Pour the blondie batter into the lined tin, making sure it is evenly spread.

*8* Remove the cream cheese filling from the freezer and carefully spoon the sugar filling and the cream cheese filling into two separate piping bags. Snip off the very end of the piping bags (or use a writing nozzle tip) and pipe alternate lines into the top of the blondie batter, then use a knife or skewer to swirl or feather them into the batter. Bake for 30 minutes.

*9* Once removed from the oven, the middle should still wobble. Leave to cool completely in the tin. Chill for at least 6 hours (preferably overnight) before cutting into squares or rectangles.

# CARROT CAKE CRUMBLE BLONDIES

Carrot cake combined with cream cheese, combined with crumble, combined with blondie. Could this be the winter warmer recipe of dreams?! Serve hot with custard or cold with pouring cream.

## INGREDIENTS

*Makes 8–10*

**Cream cheese filling**

45g (1½oz) full-fat cream cheese

50g (⅓ cup) icing sugar

A dash of lemon juice

2 tsp cornflour

**Crumble**

50g (3½ tbsp) unsalted butter

75g (⅔ cup) plain flour

1 tsp ground sweet cinnamon

40g (3¼ tbsp) light soft brown sugar

30g (2½ tbsp) demerara sugar

**Blondie**

220g (2 sticks) unsalted butter

125g (4½oz) white chocolate

3 eggs

125g (½ cup plus 2 tbsp) light soft brown sugar

125g (⅔ cup) caster sugar

40g (2 tbsp) golden syrup

1½ tsp mixed spice

1½ tsp ground ginger

¼ tsp salt

150g (5½oz) grated carrots

285g (2 cups plus 2 tbsp) plain flour

1 heaped tsp cornflour

200g (7oz) white chocolate chips

100g (⅔ cup) sultanas (optional)

## SPECIAL EQUIPMENT

Mixer or hand-held electric whisk

23cm (9in) square tin or 20 x 30cm (8 x 12in) rectangular tin, lined

Piping bag

1   Prepare the cream cheese filling. Using the whisk attachment on a mixer, whip the cream cheese. Add the icing sugar (no need to sift), lemon juice and the cornflour. If needed, add an extra 1 teaspoon of icing sugar at a time until it is the consistency of royal icing. Place in the freezer for later – this is best used after it has been frozen for several hours.

2   Prepare the crumble. Cut the butter into cubes and rub through the flour and cinnamon until there are small chunks of butter throughout. Add both sugars and lift gently with your fingers to combine. Set aside.

3   Preheat the oven to 180°C (160°C fan/350°F/Gas 4).

4   Using a microwave, or a bain-marie, melt the butter with the white chocolate.

5   In a mixer, combine the eggs and both sugars. Add the melted chocolate mixture and golden syrup and continue mixing. Remember to scrape the mixture around the sides and bottom of the bowl with a spatula. Add the spices, salt and grated carrots. Sift in the flour and cornflour and fold in. With a spatula, fold in 150g (5½oz) of the white chocolate chips and the sultanas, if using, with a spatula.

6   Pour half the mixture into the tin, then load a piping bag with the cream cheese filling and snip off the end. Carefully pipe lines of cream cheese filling into the batter and, using a skewer, draw circles to combine. Pour the remaining blondie batter over the top and spread out with the back of a spoon.

7   Pipe more lines of cream cheese filling in the batter and use the skewer to feather the filling. Bake for 20 minutes.

8   Sprinkle over the remaining 50g (1¾oz) white chocolate chips and spoon over the crumble. Bake for a further 15–20 minutes – the middle should still wobble when removed. Leave to cool completely in the tin, then chill in the fridge for at least 6 hours, or overnight, before cutting into squares or rectangles.

# MILLIONAIRE'S BROWNIES

If you can't decide between a millionaire's shortbread and a brownie, now you don't need to. Our classic chocolate brownie topped with soft caramel and milk chocolate is a guaranteed crowd-pleaser.

## INGREDIENTS

*Makes 8–10*

**Caramel**

180g (1½ sticks) unsalted butter

80g (6½ tbsp) caster sugar

120g (½ cup) golden syrup

397g (14oz) can of condensed milk

**Brownie**

100g (3½oz) milk chocolate

160g (1¼ sticks) unsalted butter

2 eggs

160g (¾ cup) caster sugar

65g (⅔ cup) cocoa powder

65g (½ cup) plain flour

150g (5½oz) milk chocolate chips

**Decoration**

250g (9oz) milk chocolate

15ml (1 tbsp) vegetable oil, plus a dash

60g (2¼oz) white chocolate

## SPECIAL EQUIPMENT

Mixer or hand-held electric whisk

23cm (9in) square tin or 20 x 30cm (8 x 12in) rectangular tin, lined

> **TOP TIPS** ★ If the caramel is "greasy" or the butter has started to separate, add a few spoonfuls of boiling water and mix until it comes back together. We prefer to use a mixer for this. ★ Use bake-stable chocolate chips so that they don't melt during baking.

1  The caramel can be made well in advance and stored in the fridge. In a pan on the hob, melt the butter. Add the sugar and golden syrup over a low heat and stir. Pour in the condensed milk and turn up the heat. Bring to the boil while stirring continuously – you must stir vigorously or black lumps of burnt caramel will surface. Once boiling, turn down the heat and stir until thickened and golden brown. Do not leave unattended – you must stir continuously. The longer you stir the caramel, the darker and richer it will become. This may take 15–20 minutes. Pour into a heatproof bowl and set aside.

2  Preheat the oven to 180°C (160°C fan/350°F/Gas 4).

3  Melt the milk chocolate and butter together and stir until combined. Mix the eggs and sugar together. Slowly add the melted chocolate mixture on a low-speed setting. Sift in the cocoa powder and flour, scraping down the sides of the bowl with a spatula.

4  Fold in the chocolate chips and spoon into the lined tin. Spread the batter up to the edges of the tin.

5  Bake for 20–22 minutes – the middle should still wobble when removed. Leave to cool completely in the tin, then chill for another couple of hours.

6  Spread the caramel over the top of the brownie (this may need to be reheated until warm if made previously) so the brownie is evenly covered. Chill in the fridge for 10 minutes or until the caramel is tacky.

7  Melt the milk chocolate in the microwave or in a bain-marie. Add the oil and mix together – this will prevent the chocolate from cracking. Melt the white chocolate with a dash of oil in the microwave or in a bain-marie. When the caramel is set, pour and spread the milk chocolate over the caramel. Spoon over the white chocolate in lines and use a skewer to feather together. Chill for at least 6 hours (preferably overnight), then slice into squares or rectangles to serve.

# S'MORES BROWNIES

Add to the s'mores effect by toasting the marshmallows under the grill as it helps the marshmallows expand before it toasts them. If you're not a massive cinnamon fan, omit it from the brownie batter.

## INGREDIENTS

*Makes 9*

140g (5oz) milk or dark chocolate

240g (2 sticks) unsalted butter

3 eggs

240g (1¼ cups) caster sugar

100g (1 cup) cocoa powder

3 tsp ground sweet cinnamon

100 (¾ cup) plain flour

100g (3½oz) milk chocolate chunks

5 digestive biscuits

100g (2 cups) mini marshmallows

### Topping

15g (1 tbsp) granulated sugar

15g (1 tbsp) light soft brown sugar

1 tsp ground sweet cinnamon

100g (3½oz) milk chocolate

About 80g (1½ cups) mini marshmallows

50g (1¾oz) dark chocolate, melted

1 digestive biscuit

## SPECIAL EQUIPMENT

Mixer or hand-held electric whisk

23cm (9in) square tin or 20 x 30cm (8 x 12in) rectangular tin, lined

Kitchen blowtorch (optional)

Baking tray (optional)

Piping bag (optional)

1   Preheat the oven to 200°C (180°C fan/400°F/Gas 6).

2   Melt the chocolate and butter together in a bain-marie, or in short bursts in the microwave. Mix the eggs and sugar in a mixer, or using a hand-held electric whisk. Slowly add the melted chocolate mixture, mixing on a low-speed setting.

3   Sift in the cocoa powder, cinnamon and flour and fold in by hand or on a low-speed setting. Add about 75g (2¾oz) of the chocolate chunks and stir through.

4   Pour half of the batter into the lined tin. Use a rolling pin and your fingers to break up four digestive biscuits, making sure there is a combination of larger pieces and crumbs. Spread these across the brownie batter, then pour the remaining batter on top. Crumble the remaining digestive biscuit on top and scatter over the remaining 25g (scant 1oz) of chocolate chunks.

5   Bake for 15 minutes. Meanwhile, mix the granulated sugar, light brown sugar and cinnamon together. Remove the tin from the oven and spread the mini marshmallows over the top. Sprinkle over half the cinnamon sugar and bake for another 10 minutes.

6   Leave to cool in the tin, then chill in the fridge for a few hours, preferably overnight. Cut into squares or rectangles.

7   Melt the milk chocolate gently over a bain-marie, or in short bursts in the microwave. Spoon some chocolate onto each brownie and use the back of the spoon to create an even layer. Stick a small handful of marshmallows to the chocolate (about 10g/2 tsp per brownie). Sprinkle the remaining cinnamon sugar over the brownies.

8   Use the blowtorch to lightly toast the marshmallows, or place the brownies on a baking tray under a hot grill. Remove as soon as the marshmallows have reached your desired shade!

9   Put the melted dark chocolate into a piping bag and snip off the very end. Drizzle across each brownie before crumbling the digestive biscuit on top.

# PEPPERMINT, STRAWBERRY OR ORANGE CRÈME BROWNIES

This crème recipe can be used on its own without the brownie – add a little more icing sugar until mouldable, roll out with a rolling pin and cut into shapes with pastry cutters. Dip or drizzle in chocolate, leave to set and off you go back to school to sell your goods on the stall.

## INGREDIENTS

*Makes 8–20*

270g (1⅓ cups) golden caster sugar

3 eggs

150g (5½oz) dark chocolate

270g (2 sticks plus 2 tbsp) unsalted butter

100g (1 cup) cocoa powder

120g (scant 1 cup) plain flour

100g (3½oz) milk or dark chocolate chips

### Topping

600g (5 cups) icing sugar

2 egg whites

Peppermint, strawberry or orange flavouring

Green, pink or orange gel or paste food colouring (optional)

300g (10oz) milk or dark chocolate

15ml (1 tbsp) vegetable oil

## SPECIAL EQUIPMENT

Mixer or hand-held electric whisk

23cm (9in) square tin or 20 x 30cm (8 x 12in) rectangular tin, lined

**TOP TIP ★** Wipe the knife clean between every cut to ensure the chocolate does not smear onto the middle section.

*1* Preheat the oven to 180°C (160°C fan/350°F/Gas 4).

*2* Whisk the sugar with the eggs in a mixer or using a hand-held electric whisk. In another heatproof bowl or pan, break up the dark chocolate and add the butter. Melt together in short bursts in the microwave, or over a low heat. Stir until combined and smooth.

*3* Slowly pour the melted chocolate mixture into the bowl with the whisked eggs and sugar. Mix until combined. Finally, sift in the cocoa powder and flour and hand mix, making sure to scrape around the sides of the bowl and incorporate all of the dry ingredients. Mix in the chocolate chips.

*4* Pour the mixture into the lined tin and bake for 20–25 minutes. Leave to cool, then chill in the fridge for several hours (or preferably overnight) to ensure the brownies are extra fudgy.

*5* Sift the icing sugar into a bowl and slowly whisk in the egg whites until the mixture is stiff. If the mixture is too runny, add some more icing sugar. Add a few drops of flavouring, depending on which flavour you would like – our customers love peppermint and orange crème, however, we like strawberry! Add a few drops of food colouring, if you like.

*6* Spread the crème across the top of the chilled brownie and leave to set for an hour or so – do not place in the fridge as this does not help the crème to set.

*7* Melt the chocolate in a bain-marie or in short bursts in the microwave and add the vegetable oil – this will ensure a clean cut of the chocolate once sliced. Without the oil, the chocolate will crack when cutting it. Pour all the chocolate over the crème topping, or save some to drizzle over the top once set.

*8* Leave to set, then slice into however many brownies you'd like! Drizzle with more chocolate as you wish.

# NUTELLA CORNFLAKE BROWNIES

Using cereal in baking can feel like child's play, however, there is nothing childish about these brownies. Our thick signature brownie topped with syrupy, Nutella-coated cornflakes. If you have a sweet tooth, you're going to love these!

## INGREDIENTS

*Makes 8–10*

100g (3½oz) milk chocolate

160g (1¼ sticks) unsalted butter

2 eggs

160g (¾ cup) caster sugar

65g (⅔ cup) cocoa powder

65g (½ cup) plain flour

150g (5½oz) milk or dark chocolate chips

### Cornflake topping

50g (3½ tbsp) unsalted butter

125g (½ cup) golden syrup

25g (2 tbsp) light soft brown sugar

150g (⅔ cup) Nutella

120g (4¼oz) cornflakes

## SPECIAL EQUIPMENT

Mixer or electric hand whisk

23cm (9in) square tin or 20 x 30cm (8 x 12in) rectangular tin, lined

*1* Preheat the oven to 180°C (160°C fan/350°F/Gas 4).

*2* Melt the chocolate and butter together in a bain-marie, or in short bursts in the microwave, stirring until combined.

*3* Whisk the eggs and sugar together in a mixer (or in a mixing bowl using a hand-held electric whisk). Slowly add the melted chocolate mixture while still mixing on a low-speed setting. Sift in the cocoa powder and flour, scraping down the sides of the bowl with a spatula before re-mixing.

*4* Fold in 120g (4¼oz) of the chocolate chips with a spatula and then spoon the batter into the lined tin. Spread the batter up to the edges of the tin and scatter the remaining chocolate chips over the top. Bake for 23 minutes.

*5* While the brownie is baking, melt together the butter, golden syrup and sugar, then add the Nutella. Measure the cornflakes into a large bowl and pour the liquid over the top. Use a spoon to mix everything together, ensuring all of the cornflakes are completely coated.

*6* Remove the brownie from the oven and spoon over the Nutella cornflake mix. Push the cornflakes up to the edges of the tin and evenly spread with the back of a spoon.

*7* Bake for a further 10 minutes. Remove from the oven and leave to cool completely in the tin. Chilli in the fridge for at least 6 hours before cutting into squares or triangles.

> TOP TIP ★ We recommend using bake-stable chocolate chips in the brownie batter so that they keep their shape during baking.

# HALF & HALF BLONDIE BROWNIES

The best of both worlds – our blondie brownie is a bestseller. It does take a bit more time than the usual recipe as the brownie is double baked, however, this hybrid is worth the wait! Our two classic recipes joining together for an ultimate battle of the blondie vs. brownie, but which is your favourite?

## INGREDIENTS

*Makes 9–10*

### Brownie

90g (3¼oz) milk chocolate, plus 150g (5½oz) chunks

160g (1¼ sticks) unsalted butter

2 eggs

160g (¾ cup) caster sugar

65g (⅔ cup) cocoa powder

65g (½ cup) plain flour

300g (1¼ cups) spread, such as Nutella, Lotus Biscoff or white chocolate hazelnut crème, melted

### Blondie

80g (2¾oz) white chocolate

120g (1 stick) unsalted butter

2 eggs

40g (3¼ tbsp) light soft brown sugar

80g (6½ tbsp) caster sugar

1 tsp vanilla extract

30g (1½ tbsp) golden syrup

1 tbsp cornflour

200g (scant 1½ cups) plain flour

150g (5½oz) white chocolate chunks, plus extra for topping

### Decoration

50g (1¾oz) white chocolate, plus extra for topping

50g (1¾oz) milk chocolate, plus extra for topping

## SPECIAL EQUIPMENT

Mixer or hand-held electric whisk

23cm (9in) square tin or 20 x 30cm (8 x 12in) rectangular tin, lined
Piping bags

*1* Preheat the oven to 180°C (160°C fan/350°F/Gas 4).

*2* Melt the milk chocolate and butter together in a bain-marie, or in short bursts in the microwave, stirring until combined.

*3* Whisk the eggs and sugar in a mixer (or in a mixing bowl using a hand-held electric whisk). Slowly add the melted chocolate mixture while still mixing on a low-speed setting. Sift in the cocoa powder and flour and fold in by hand or on a low-speed setting, remembering to scrape down the sides of the bowl with a spatula. Mix in the 150g (5½oz) milk chocolate chunks.

*4* Pour into the lined tin, spread level and bake for 22 minutes.

*5* While the brownie layer is baking, melt the white chocolate and butter together and stir until combined.

*6* Whisk the eggs, both sugars, the vanilla extract and golden syrup in a mixer (or in a mixing bowl using a hand-held electric whisk). Slowly add the melted chocolate mixture while still mixing on a low-speed setting. Sift in the cornflour and flour and fold in by hand or on a low-speed setting, remembering to scrape down the sides of the bowl with a spatula. Mix in the white chocolate chunks.

*7* Once the brownie has finished baking, remove from the oven. If adding spread, leave the brownie to cool, then pour over the melted spread. Chill for 30 minutes and continue with the blondie batter. If not using spread, pour the blondie batter on top of the hot brownie and, using the back of a spoon, spread it out evenly, then scatter a few more white chocolate chunks on top. Bake for a further 24 minutes.

*8* Cool in the tin, then chill in the fridge for several hours or overnight. Cut into squares, then melt the white and milk chocolates separately, load into two piping bags, snip off the tips and drizzle across the top of each brownie. Decorate with chunks of milk and white chocolate, if you like.

# OREO LOAF CAKE

This all-in-one cake is the perfect weekend bake – throw everything into one bowl, pour into one tin and you're 40 minutes away from the most heavenly cookies and cream sponge you will ever taste. Enjoy a slice on its own with minimal washing up (yay!) or grab another packet of those famous black and white cookies and get decorating! Best served along with a pot of tea and some gossip with your best pals on a Sunday afternoon.

## INGREDIENTS

Serves 4–6

385g (13oz) Oreos (2½ packets)

140g (1 stick plus 1 tbsp) unsalted butter

70ml (⅓ cup) buttermilk

1 egg

½ tsp bicarbonate of soda

2 tsp baking powder

20g (¼ cup) cocoa powder

Dash of milk

100g (¾ cup) icing sugar

### Buttercream

100g (6½ tbsp) unsalted butter

180g (1⅓ cup) icing sugar

Vanilla extract, to taste

3 Oreos, crushed to crumbs

### Decoration

75g (3oz) chocolate (we used 25g/1oz milk, 25g/1oz white and 25g/1oz dark chocolate)

10 whole Oreos, plus 2 crushed

## SPECIAL EQUIPMENT

Food processor (preferable) or rolling pin

900g (2lb) loaf tin, lined

Piping bags and large piping nozzle

Mixer or hand-held electric whisk

---

1   Preheat the oven to 180°C (160°C fan/350°F/Gas 4).

2   Crush the Oreos in a food processor, or place into a bowl or bag and use a rolling pin to crush the cookies, leaving some larger pieces. Place into the mixing bowl.

3   Melt the butter in short bursts in the microwave or in a saucepan over a gentle heat. Pour over the crushed cookies.

4   Next, add the buttermilk and egg to the mixing bowl, then sift in the bicarbonate of soda, baking powder and cocoa powder. Mix until fully incorporated, then add a dash of milk to loosen the batter slightly.

5   Pour the batter into the lined tin, spread evenly and bake for 40–45 minutes. Leave to cool slightly in the tin, then turn onto a wire rack to cool completely.

6   Mix the icing sugar with a small amount of water (depending on how thick you'd like the icing). Load into a piping bag, snip off the tip and drizzle the icing over the top of the loaf.

7   To make the buttercream, whip the butter in a mixer or with a hand-held electric whisk until pale and fluffy. Add the icing sugar and vanilla extract to taste and mix.

8   Gently fold the crushed Oreos into the buttercream, using a spatula. Load into a piping bag with a large piping nozzle and pipe along the middle of the top of the loaf cake.

9   Gently melt the milk chocolate in a bain-marie or in short bursts in the microwave and, using a cocktail stick, dip five Oreos into the melted chocolate and leave to dry. Melt the white chocolate and drizzle over the chocolate-dipped cookies, then sprinkle over small pieces of dark chocolate. Decorate the cake with the chocolate-dipped Oreos, the remaining whole Oreos and the crushed Oreos.

# APPLE & CINNAMON LOAF CAKE

Packed with autumnal flavour, this simple recipe will leave your kitchen smelling heavenly all year round! Just add cups of tea and friends to make this the perfect get-together treat.

## INGREDIENTS

*Serves 6*

150g (1 stick plus 2 tbsp) unsalted butter

150g (¾ cup packed) light soft brown sugar

2 eggs

2 tbsp buttermilk

2 tsp ground sweet cinnamon

150g (1 cup plus 2 tbsp) self-raising flour

**Filling**

1 Bramley apple

25g (1½ tbsp) unsalted butter

1 tsp ground sweet cinnamon

30g (2½ tbsp) demerara sugar

**Decoration**

100g (6½ tbsp) unsalted butter

200g (1⅓ cups) icing sugar

Vanilla extract, to taste

Caramel, for drizzling (optional)

Ground sweet cinnamon, for dusting

## SPECIAL EQUIPMENT

Mixer or hand-held electric whisk

900g (2lb) loaf tin, lined

Angled metal palette knife (optional)

Piping bag and nozzle (optional)

**TOP TIP** ★ Finely slice a cooking apple and bake on a baking tray alongside the cake for 50 minutes. Leave to cool for 5–10 minutes until dried and crispy and use for decoration.

*1* Preheat the oven to 180°C (160°C fan/350°F/Gas 4).

*2* Put the butter and sugar into the bowl of a mixer (or use a mixing bowl and a hand-held electric whisk). Using the paddle attachment, cream together on a high-speed setting until combined. Add the eggs, one by one, on a low-speed setting.

*3* Add the buttermilk and cinnamon and then sift in the flour. Mix until just combined, scraping down the sides of the bowl with a spatula and re-mixing. Spoon the batter into the lined tin and spread evenly.

*4* Bake for 50–60 minutes, or until the sponge bounces back when pressed or a cocktail stick inserted into the middle comes out clean. Leave to cool in the tin for 10 minutes, then transfer the loaf cake (still in its liner) onto a wire rack to cool completely (this may take 1–2 hours).

*5* While the sponge is cooling, prepare the spiced apple filling. Peel and core the apple, then chop it into small cubes. Melt the butter in a pan over a medium heat and add the cubed apple with a couple of tablespoons of water.

*6* Spoon over the cinnamon and demerara sugar, stir the mixture and replace the lid. Stir every couple of minutes until the apple has started to soften (but isn't mushy). Remove from the heat and leave to cool.

*7* Prepare a batch of **VANILLA BUTTERCREAM** following the instructions on page 200 and using the quantities listed here.

*8* Once the cake has cooled, remove it from the liner and either spread the buttercream over the top of the loaf cake with an angled palette knife or a loaded piping bag with a nozzle of your choice.

*9* Spoon over the cooled apple mixture, drizzle with caramel and decorate with dried apples (see Tip), if using, and a dusting of cinnamon.

# MAPLE & PECAN LOAF CAKE

Fluffy, syrupy sponge cake with lashings of cream cheese buttercream, this recipe feels like autumn but also like we may be eating it all year round...

## INGREDIENTS

*Serves 4–6*

140g (1 stick plus 1 tbsp) unsalted butter

140g (⅔ cup packed) light soft brown sugar

2 eggs

140g (1 cup) self-raising flour

2 tbsp buttermilk

100g (3½oz) maple syrup

100g (3½oz) pecans, chopped into small pieces, plus extra to decorate

### Cream cheese buttercream

100g (6½ tbsp) unsalted butter

50g (1¾oz) maple syrup

50g (1¾oz) full-fat cream cheese

200g (1⅔ cups) icing sugar

## SPECIAL EQUIPMENT

Mixer or hand-held electric whisk

900g (2lb) loaf tin, lined

Piping bag and small closed star nozzle

*1*  Preheat the oven to 180°C (160°C fan/350°F/Gas 4).

*2*  Put the butter and sugar into the bowl of a mixer (or use a mixing bowl and a hand-held electric whisk). Using the paddle attachment, cream together on a high-speed setting until fluffy. Add the eggs, one by one, on a low-speed setting.

*3*  Sift in the flour and measure out the buttermilk and maple syrup. Add to the bowl and combine slowly until the mixture has come together. Add the chopped pecans and fold in by hand or on a low-speed setting.

*4*  Spoon the batter into the lined tin and use the back of a spoon to spread it out evenly. Bake for 50–60 minutes, or until a cocktail stick inserted into the middle comes out clean. Leave to cool in the tin for 10 minutes, then transfer the loaf cake in its liner to a wire rack to cool completely (this may take 1–2 hours).

*5*  While the cake is cooling, prepare the cream cheese buttercream. In a mixer fitted with the paddle attachment, cream the butter, maple syrup and cream cheese together for 5–10 minutes. Sift in the icing sugar and mix on a low-speed setting until combined. Scrape down the sides of the bowl and re-mix. Chill until ready to decorate.

*6*  Once the cake has cooled, remove from the liner and re-mix the buttercream. Load into a piping bag fitted with a small closed star nozzle and pipe along the top of the cake. Decorate with more chopped pecans.

> **TOP TIP** ★ You can also decorate the cake with pieces of pecan brittle, as we've done in the photo. Add 250g (1¼ cups) golden caster sugar to a saucepan with a splash of water and let it caramelize. Stir in 150g (5½oz) pecans. Quickly pour onto a tray lined with greaseproof paper and leave to set. Break into pieces and use to decorate instead of, or as well as, the chopped pecans.

# SCHOOL CAKE

School cake has made a big comeback: from 1990s school dinners to appearing in every cake shop in the UK, this versatile sponge cake, with its thick water icing, is always a sellout in our shops.

## INGREDIENTS

*Makes 2 cakes or 8 slices*

200g (1¾ sticks) unsalted butter

200g (1 cup) caster sugar

3 eggs

200g (scant 1½ cups) self-raising flour

**Decoration**

300g (2 cups plus 2 tbsp) icing sugar

Sprinkles of your choice

## SPECIAL EQUIPMENT

Mixer or hand-held electric whisk

2 x 900g (2lb) loaf tins, lined

### TOP TIPS

★ Save any cut off cake for a later date – it can be frozen or made into cake pops.

★ To turn into a lemon cake, use 5–10 drops of lemon extract in both the cake batter and the icing.

★ To make a cherry Bakewell version, add 5 drops of almond extract and 100g (3½oz) glacé cherries to the batter, and once the cake is iced, decorate with 50g (1¾oz) toasted flaked almonds and 50g (1¾oz) glacé cherries.

*1* Preheat the oven to 200°C (180°C fan/400°F/Gas 6).

*2* In the bowl of a mixer (or use a mixing bowl and a hand-held electric whisk), combine the butter and sugar together on a high-speed setting for 5 minutes. Add the eggs, one by one, on a low-speed setting.

*3* Sift the flour into the bowl, remembering to scrape down the sides of the bowl with a spatula before mixing until just combined.

*4* Weigh 400g (14oz) of cake batter into each lined tin, then spread it level. Bake both cakes for 30 minutes, or until a cocktail stick inserted into the middle comes out clean. Leave to cool slightly in the tins, then transfer the cakes in their liners to a wire rack to cool completely.

*5* Once cold, remove the cakes from the liners and trim the tops of the cakes using a sharp knife or a cake leveller.

*6* Weigh out the icing sugar into a bowl and add a drop of water at a time until it turns into a thick paste. Keep adding small amounts of water until only very slightly runny. For super thick icing, we make ours in a mixer rather than by hand and leave it to set overnight.

*7* Spoon the icing over the top of each cake, remembering to push it up to the edges. It doesn't matter if the icing runs over the edge. Quickly add sprinkles before the icing starts to set. Leave to set at room temperature until the icing has hardened – preferably overnight. Slice and enjoy!

# PARTY TREATS
# & SWEETS

# INDIVIDUAL MINI VICTORIA SPONGES

Individually gift wrapped or laid out on the table for a homemade afternoon tea, these cute Victoria sponges are built from a sheet cake and cookie cutters!

## INGREDIENTS

*Makes 4 small cakes*

250g (9oz) raspberries

1 heaped tbsp cornflour

360g (3 sticks plus 1 tbsp) unsalted butter

360g (1¾ cups) caster sugar

6 eggs

360g (2¾ cups plus 1 tbsp) self-raising flour

### Filling

250g (2 sticks) unsalted butter

400g (3⅓ cups) icing sugar

5 drops of vanilla extract

8 tsp raspberry jam

### Decoration

Fruit, such as raspberries, strawberries and blueberries

Icing sugar, for dusting

## SPECIAL EQUIPMENT

20 x 40cm (8 x 16in) baking tray, lined

Mixer or hand-held electric whisk

8cm (3¼in) round cookie cutters

Piping bag and star nozzle

4 x thick 12cm (4½in) cake cards

*1* Preheat the oven to 180°C (160°C fan/350°F/Gas 4).

*2* In a bowl, coat the raspberries in the cornflour and stir until completely covered, trying not to break up the berries. Set aside.

*3* Cream the butter and sugar together in a mixer until white and doubled in size. On a low-speed setting, add the eggs, one by one. Sift in the flour and fold in, either with a spatula or on a low-speed setting. Carefully fold in the coated raspberries.

*4* Pour the mixture into the lined baking tray and spread up to the sides. Bake for 33–35 minutes until the sponge bounces back when touched. Leave to cool slightly in the tin for 5 minutes, then invert onto a large wire rack and leave to cool completely.

*5* To prepare the buttercream filling, whip the butter in a bowl on a high-speed setting until whitened. Sift in the icing sugar and add the vanilla extract. Use a spatula to mix again.

*6* Take the cookie cutter and press into the sponge cake. Repeat until you have 12 circles of sponge. You can mix the excess sponge with extra buttercream to make cake pops. This mix can also be frozen.

*7* Load a piping bag fitted with a star nozzle with the vanilla buttercream and pipe small blobs onto a cake card. Stick down one sponge circle and repeat with the remaining cake cards.

*8* Spoon 1 teaspoon of jam onto the middle of eight of the sponges. Pipe small whips of buttercream around the outside of the four base sponges and one in the middle. Take the other four circles of sponge with jam on and arrange neatly on top of each base sponge. Chill in the fridge for 10 minutes. Repeat piping around the edge and middle of each sponge before adding the final sponges, upside down, to achieve a flat top. Chill for another 10 minutes.

*9* Arrange the raspberries, strawberries and blueberries on the top of the mini cakes, attaching with excess buttercream. Dust the sponges and fruit with icing sugar.

# NO-BAKE CHOCOLATE ORANGE ROCKY ROAD

Ganache in a rocky road just makes all the difference. This chocolate orange one is stuffed with Jaffas and Terry's Chocolate orange – a crunchy but chewy, citrus delight.

## INGREDIENTS

*Serves 8–10*

1 Terry's Chocolate Orange

400g (14oz) digestive biscuits

125g (1 stick) unsalted butter

150g (⅔ cup) golden syrup

350g (12oz) milk chocolate

5–10 drops of orange extract

60ml (¼ cup) double cream

8 Jaffa Cakes

120g (2½ cups) mini marshmallows

**Topping**

300g (10oz) milk chocolate

20ml (4 tsp) vegetable oil

Sprinkles (optional)

Chocolate curls (optional)

## SPECIAL EQUIPMENT

Food processor (optional)

20 x 30cm (8 x 12in) tin, lined

*1* Put the Terry's Chocolate Orange in the freezer and leave until frozen. Crush the digestive biscuits in a food processor, or place into a bowl or bag and use a rolling pin to crush the biscuits, leaving some larger pieces. Set aside.

*2* In the microwave, melt the butter and golden syrup together. Pour in the crushed digestive biscuits and stir until they are completely coated.

*3* Melt the milk chocolate in a bain-maire, or in short bursts in the microwave, then pour in the orange extract and double cream and combine. Pour into the crushed digestive mixture and stir.

*4* Cut the Jaffa Cakes in half. Remove the frozen Chocolate Orange from the freezer and add 100g (3½oz) of the segments, the Jaffa Cake pieces and the marshmallows to the chocolate and biscuit mixture. Stir again until completely coated.

*5* Pour or spoon the mixture into the lined tin and use a spoon to push it evenly up to the edges of the tin. Chill in the fridge to set.

*6* Melt the milk chocolate in a bain-marie, or in short bursts in the microwave, and stir in the oil until combined, then pour evenly over the rocky road. Decorate with more Chocolate Orange pieces as well as sprinkles and chocolate curls, if using. Chill in the fridge until set, then use a sharp knife to cut into squares or rectangles.

# NO-BAKE JAMMIE DODGER ROCKY ROAD

Biscuity, sweet, white chocolate rocky road with bursts of jam throughout and topped with more Jammie Dodger biscuits. We've transformed a favourite childhood biscuit into your new favourite rocky road flavour.

## INGREDIENTS

*Serves 8–10*

400g (14oz) digestive biscuits

100g (3½oz) mini Jammie Dodgers

80g (5 tbsp) unsalted butter

150g (⅔ cup) golden syrup

400g (14oz) white chocolate

60ml (4 tbsp) double cream

120g (2½ cups) mini marshmallows

100g (3½oz) white chocolate chips

150g (5½oz) raspberry jam

### Topping

450g (1lb) white chocolate

20ml (4 tsp) vegetable oil

Mini Jammie Dodgers

White chocolate chips

Freeze-dried raspberries (optional)

## SPECIAL EQUIPMENT

Food processor or rolling pin

20 x 30cm (8 x 12in) tin, lined

Piping bag

*1* Crush the digestive biscuits in a food processor, or place into a bowl or bag and use a rolling pin to crush the biscuits, leaving some larger pieces. Break up half of the Jammie Dodgers with your fingers and leave half whole. Mix all the biscuits together and set aside.

*2* In a heatproof bowl in the microwave, melt the butter and golden syrup together. Add all the mixed (broken and whole) biscuits. Stir together with a spatula until combined, scraping around the sides to make sure everything is mixed in.

*3* Melt the white chocolate in a bain-maire, or in short bursts in the microwave and combine with the cream. Add to the biscuit mixture and stir again.

*4* Add the marshmallows and chocolate chips and stir again until evenly distributed and coated.

*5* Pour or spoon the mixture into the lined tin and use a spoon to push it evenly up to the edges of the tin. Load the raspberry jam into a piping bag and snip off the tip. Use the end of a clean spoon to make shallow holes all over the rocky road. Pipe the jam into the holes and put into the fridge to chill.

*6* To make the topping, melt the chocolate in a bain-marie, or in short bursts in the microwave, and stir in the oil until combined, then pour evenly over the rocky road. Pipe any leftover jam onto the melted white chocolate and swirl in using a skewer or cocktail stick.

*7* Decorate with more mini Jammie Dodger biscuits and white chocolate chips. If using, fill in the gaps with some freeze-dried raspberry pieces. Chill in the fridge until set, then use a sharp knife to cut into squares or rectangles.

# TOFFEE CRISP ROCKY ROAD

Our classic rocky road recipe is topped with a Rice Krispie and caramel layer, chocolate and Toffee Crisps to decorate. An ode to the underrated chocolate bar; you won't be able to resist this crunchy yet chewy no-bake. We've even melted marshmallows into this recipe, so the biscuit is extra soft. Perfect for a party dessert table!

## INGREDIENTS

*Makes 10–20 pieces (depending on how chunky they are!)*

400g (14oz) digestive biscuits

350g (12oz) milk chocolate

125g (1 stick) unsalted butter

125g (½ cup) golden syrup

120g (4¼oz) Rice Krispies

130g (2½ cups) mini marshmallows

200g (7oz) store-bought caramel and 100g (3½oz) white chocolate OR caramel (see below)

### Caramel (optional)

90g (5½ tbsp) unsalted butter

40g (3½ tbsp) caster sugar

60g (⅓ cup) golden syrup

½ x 397g (14oz) can of condensed milk

### Topping

400g (14oz) milk chocolate

25ml (5 tsp) vegetable oil

5 Toffee Crisp chocolate bars, chopped

## SPECIAL EQUIPMENT

Food processor or rolling pin

23cm (9in) square tin or 20 x 30cm (8 x 12in) rectangular tin, lined

1 Crush the digestive biscuits in a food processor, or place into a bowl or bag and use a rolling pin to crush the biscuits, leaving some larger pieces. Tip into a bowl.

2 In a microwave or a pan on the hob, gently melt the chocolate, butter and golden syrup together. Stir until combined.

3 Pour the crushed digestives and half the Rice Krispies into the chocolate mixture and stir until completely coated.

4 Place the mini marshmallows into a bowl with 1 teaspoon of water and stir to coat. Heat in the microwave for 20–30 seconds or until they have expanded, then melted. Stir into the chocolate and biscuit mixture until evenly distributed and coated. Spoon the mixture into the lined tin and press down in an even layer with the back of a spoon. Set aside.

5 Melt the store-bought caramel and white chocolate together in a bain-marie, or in the microwave in short bursts, if using.

6 Alternatively, If making the caramel, melt the butter in a saucepan on the hob. Add the sugar and golden syrup over a low heat and stir. Pour in the condensed milk and turn up the heat. Bring to the boil while stirring continuously – you must stir vigorously or black lumps of caramel will surface. Once boiling, turn down the heat and stir until thickened and golden brown. Do not leave unattended. The longer you stir the caramel, the darker and richer it will become. This may take 15–20 minutes. Remove from the heat and set aside to cool slightly.

7 Add the remaining Rice Krispies to the caramel and stir to combine. Pour over the top of the rocky road in an even layer and chill in the fridge to set.

8 For the topping, melt the milk chocolate over a bain-marie, or in short bursts in the microwave, and stir in the oil until combined, then pour it over the Rice Krispie layer. Top with Toffee Crisp pieces. Leave to set, then cut into a size of your choice to serve.

# NO-BAKE MILLIONAIRE'S ROCKY ROAD

When your faves come together! Whether it's in the biscuit tin, wrapped up in lunchboxes or an after tea treat, this millionaire's shortbread rocky road will become a new family favourite.

## INGREDIENTS

*Serves 8–10*

300g (10oz) digestive biscuits

200g (7oz) shortbread fingers

120g (2½ cups) mini marshmallows

80g (5 tbsp) unsalted butter

150g (⅔ cup) golden syrup

400g (14oz) milk chocolate

60ml (4 tbsp) double cream

200g (7oz) soft caramel (see page 150)

### Topping

450g (1lb) milk chocolate

30ml (6 tsp) vegetable oil

100g (3½oz) white chocolate

50g (1¾oz) caramel pieces (optional)

## SPECIAL EQUIPMENT

Food processor or rolling pin

20 x 30cm (8 x 12in) tin, lined

Piping bags

Skewer

1   Crush the digestive biscuits in a food processor, or place into a bowl or bag and use a rolling pin to crush the biscuits, leaving some larger pieces. Break up the shortbread fingers into large pieces and stir together with the digestives in a heatproof bowl. Add the marshmallows. Set aside.

2   In another heatproof bowl, in the microwave, melt the butter and golden syrup. Stir together and pour over the biscuit mixture to coat thoroughly.

3   Melt the chocolate in short bursts in the microwave and combine with the cream. Pour into the biscuit and marshmallow mixture and stir until completely coated.

4   Pour or spoon the mixture into the lined tin and use a spoon to push it evenly up to the edges of the tin. Use the end of a spoon to make deep and shallow holes throughout the mixture.

5   Load a piping bag with 150g (5½oz) of the caramel and pipe some into each hole. Chill in the fridge.

6   Melt the milk chocolate over a bain-marie, or in short bursts in the microwave, and stir in 20ml (4 tsp) of the oil. In a separate bowl, melt the white chocolate and stir in the remaining 10ml (2 tsp) of oil, then load into a piping bag. In another bowl, loosen the remaining 50g (1¾oz) of caramel in the microwave and add into another piping bag.

7   Remove the rocky road from the fridge and evenly pour over the melted milk chocolate. Pipe on alternate lines of white chocolate and caramel. Use a skewer to carefully feather the chocolate and caramel together, making sure not to bring any of the biscuit to the surface. Scatter over caramel pieces to decorate, if using.

8   Chill in the fridge to set, then use a sharp knife to cut into squares or rectangles.

# SEA SALT FUDGE

Smooth, creamy, salty and sweet, this is the perfect tea time treat or party favour. If you don't have double cream, you can swap it for full-fat milk, which will make a slightly less rich fudge.

## INGREDIENTS

*Makes 20–40 pieces*

2 x 397g (14oz) cans of condensed milk

200ml (scant 1 cup) double cream

900g (4½ cups) granulated sugar

240g (2 sticks) unsalted butter

Sea salt, to taste

## SPECIAL EQUIPMENT

Sugar thermometer (optional)

Mixer or hand-held electric whisk

23cm (9in) square tin or 20 x 30cm (8 x 12in) rectangular tin, lined

*1* Put the condensed milk, cream, sugar and butter into a saucepan and stir over a low heat until melted and combined.

*2* Turn up the heat and allow the mixture to come to the boil, stirring continuously so the mixture does not catch on the bottom of the pan. Once bubbling, turn the heat down slightly but continue to stir.

*3* The mixture should become darker as you continue to stir. Use a sugar thermometer to check the temperature, then once the temperature hits "soft ball stage" between 112°C (234°F) and 115°C (239°F), remove from the heat. Add a small amount of sea salt to taste and stir once. If you don't have a sugar thermometer, you can also check the sugar has reached this temperature by dropping a small amount into a glass of cold water – it should form a ball when it is ready. If the mixture is stringy or thread-like, it needs cooking for longer.

*4* Leave to cool without touching the fudge. Once the fudge has cooled to 60°C (140°F), pour into a mixer fitted with the paddle attachment and set to a low-speed setting, or use a mixing bowl and a hand-held electric whisk to beat for 3–4 minutes. This will break up the sugar crystals and will make for a smooth, melt-in-your-mouth fudge. The fudge should no longer be glossy and smooth but dull.

*5* Pour the fudge into the lined tin, sprinkle with sea salt to taste and leave to cool and set for 1 hour. Cut and serve.

### Note

Cooking with hot sugar can be extremely dangerous. Please wear protection if required!

# MINI EGG FUDGE

This really simple fudge recipe would usually only call for two ingredients – condensed milk and chocolate – if we hadn't sprinkled some pastel colours throughout the recipe! Leave the rest of the ingredients out if you want a quick, easy and delicious chocolate fudge or add as many extras as you like. If you can't get hold of Mini Eggs, try another chocolate to make this a year-round treat.

## INGREDIENTS

*Makes 20–80 pieces (depending on how it is cut)*

2 x 397g (14oz) cans of condensed milk

600g (1lb 5oz) white chocolate

2 tsp vanilla extract

Oil-based food colourings – we used pink, yellow, orange and mint-green

200g (7oz) milk chocolate

300g (10oz) Mini Eggs, plus 50g (1¾oz) crushed, for topping

30g (1oz) sprinkles (optional)

## SPECIAL EQUIPMENT

23cm (9in) square or 20 x 30cm (8 x 12in) rectangular tin, lined

Piping bags

*1* Pour 1½ cans of condensed milk into a heatproof bowl or saucepan with the white chocolate and either melt in the microwave in short bursts, or gently melt on the hob. Add the vanilla extract and mix with a spoon or spatula until fully incorporated.

*2* Split the fudge evenly between four bowls and add a few drops of oil-based food colouring to each one until your desired shades are achieved.

*3* Repeat step 1 with the remaining half can of condensed milk and the milk chocolate.

*4* If you'd like some texture in your fudge, use a rolling pin to crush some of the whole Mini Eggs.

*5* Once the coloured fudges and milk chocolate fudge are cool (so as not to melt the Mini Eggs), spread a few spoonfuls of each coloured fudge into the bottom of the lined tin. Then, add a layer of the milk chocolate, before sprinkling with the Mini Eggs.

*6* Place the remaining coloured chocolate fudges into four piping bags and snip off the ends. Pipe the colours in lines over the Mini Eggs/fudge in the tin – there should be enough left for two rows on top of each other.

*7* Use a knife or a cocktail stick to carefully feather a pattern through the fudge, then sprinkle some crushed Mini Eggs and sprinkles, if using, over the top, making sure the feathered pattern can still be seen.

*8* Chill in the fridge for 3–4 hours, then cut and refrigerate again until ready to serve.

# BROWNIE SCOTCH EGGS

For this recipe, you'll create a classic brownie dough and mould it around a chocolate egg. Dip your eggs in melted chocolate, roll them in crushed chocolates, biscuits or sprinkles, or dust them in cocoa powder - a perfect Easter treat.

## INGREDIENTS

Makes 6

3 eggs

280g (1⅓ cups) caster sugar

150g (5½oz) milk or dark chocolate

270g (2 sticks plus 2 tbsp) unsalted butter

100g (1 cup) cocoa powder

120g (scant 1 cup) plain flour

6 chocolate eggs, such as Creme Eggs or Galaxy Caramel Eggs (or any circular chocolate like Ferrero Rocher)

### Decoration (optional)

200g (7oz) milk, white or dark chocolate, depending on taste

20ml (4 tsp) vegetable oil (leave this out if you'd like the chocolate very firm on the outside)

100g (3½oz) crushed Mini Eggs per egg

25g (1oz) chocolate curls per egg

3 crushed Oreos per egg

30g (1oz) sprinkles

## SPECIAL EQUIPMENT

23cm (9in) square tin or 20 x 30cm (8 x 12in) rectangular baking tin or 20cm (8in) round cake tin, lined

Mixer with a dough hook (preferably) or hand-held electric whisk

Baking tray

Baking parchment

1  Preheat the oven to 180°C (160°C fan/350°F/Gas 4).

2  Whisk the eggs and caster sugar together using a hand-held electric whisk or mixer on a medium speed for 1–2 minutes.

3  Place the chocolate and butter into a bowl or saucepan and slowly melt together in the microwave or on the hob, then mix until combined. Slowly pour the mixture into the whisked eggs and combine on a low-speed setting.

4  Sift in the cocoa powder and flour and mix in using a spatula. The brownie batter should be smooth and glossy. Pour evenly into the lined tin and bake for 25 minutes. Cool in the tin, then chill in the fridge for a couple of hours.

5  Cut the brownie into small pieces and place into a bowl. Using a mixer fitted with the dough hook or a hand-held electric whisk, mix until a dough forms. (The brownie dough may be more resistant to an electric whisk compared to a mixer.)

6  Weigh out 175g (6oz) of brownie dough per chocolate egg. Use your hands to mould the brownie dough around each egg. Place on a baking tray and chill in the fridge for 30 minutes.

7  Roll the eggs between your hands again to ensure the flat edge the eggs have formed while in the fridge have become round again. Return to the fridge for another 30 minutes until firm.

8  Melt the chocolate in a pan on the hob or in the microwave in short bursts. If using, mix in the vegetable oil. Spread the Mini Eggs or your chosen chocolate on a sheet of baking parchment. Using gloved hands, dip each egg into the melted chocolate.

9  Once the chocolate has started to dry, roll the eggs in your chosen chocolate coating. Use the bottom of the baking parchment to manipulate the chocolate coating, pressing it into the sides of the brownie Scotch eggs from underneath. Chill in the fridge for another 20–30 minutes or until you are ready to serve.

# SUGAR COOKIES

The simplest but most delicious biscuits, topped with that water icing we all love!

## INGREDIENTS

*Makes about 12*

150g (1 stick plus 2 tbsp) unsalted butter

150g (⅔ cup) caster sugar

1 egg

5 drops of vanilla extract

350g (2¾ cups) plain flour, plus extra for dusting

Pinch of salt

1 tsp baking powder

### Icing

200g (1⅔ cups) icing sugar

Pink gel food colouring

Sprinkles of your choice

## SPECIAL EQUIPMENT

Mixer or hand-held electric whisk

8cm (3¼in) round cookie cutter (or any cookie cutter)

2 baking trays, lined

Piping bag

### TOP TIPS

★ We prefer to chill the dough before it is rolled and cut out as the cookies hold their shape better when transferring to the baking trays.

★ There are lots of ways to ice a sugar cookie, like piping a thin line of icing around the edge of the cookie, setting it and then "flooding" it with wetter icing. You can also apply the icing with a spoon.

*1* Whip the butter and sugar together until creamy in a mixer (or use a mixing bowl and a hand-held electric whisk). Add the egg and vanilla extract and mix on a low-speed setting until combined.

*2* Sift in the flour, salt and baking powder and mix again until a dough forms. If it feels too sticky, add another tablespoon of flour until stiffened. Remove from the bowl and knead together into a ball. You may need to use extra flour on your hands and the work surface to prevent sticking. Wrap in cling film and chill in the fridge for at least 30 minutes.

*3* Preheat the oven to 190°C (170°C fan/375°F/Gas 5).

*4* Split the chilled dough in half. Scatter more flour over your work surface and use a rolling pin to evenly roll out the dough.

*5* Cut into round cookies using the cookie cutter and carefully use an angled spatula to lift onto the lined baking trays, being careful to keep their shape and ensuring they do not touch each other.

*6* Bake for 13 minutes. If your oven has a hot spot, you may want to turn the cookies round halfway through. Leave to cool completely on the baking trays.

*7* Prepare your icing either by hand or in a mixer. Put the icing sugar in a bowl and add a couple of drops of water at a time, while mixing on a low-speed setting. Add a little pink food colouring and mix again. The icing should be thick but still slowly drop off a spoon.

*8* Load the icing into a piping bag and snip off the end. Start from the centre and pipe outwards in a tight swirl. Pick the cookie up and, keeping it upright, shake from side to side so the icing settles. Decorate with sprinkles and leave to set.

# NUTELLA CRUNCH BARS

What is better than the childhood nostalgia of a Rice Krispie cake? This simple yet delicious recipe from your school days can be the base of an unlimited amount of flavour combinations. Swap the Nutella and Maltesers for a sauce or topping of your choice!

## INGREDIENTS

*Serves 8–20*

120g (2½ cups) mini marshmallows

50g (3½ tbsp) unsalted butter

50g (2½ tbsp) golden syrup

480g (1lb 1oz) milk chocolate

150g (5½oz) Rice Krispies or crisped rice cereal

350g (1½ cups) Nutella

About 100 Maltesers, plus extra to decorate (optional)

800g (1lb 12oz) white chocolate

40ml (2½ tbsp) vegetable oil, plus a dash

## SPECIAL EQUIPMENT

23cm (9in) square tin or 20 x 30cm (8 x 12in) rectangular tin, lined

Piping bag

> **TOP TIPS ★** This recipe is extremely adaptable. Try fillings like white chocolate spread or Lotus Biscoff in between the Rice Krispie layer and the chocolate, or different chocolates for layered, chunky slices with interesting cross-sections, or switch the milk chocolate in the Rice Krispie layer to white chocolate!
> ★ The Maltesers will start to disintegrate when exposed to air, so these crunch bars or squares are best served immediately after cutting.

1   Place the marshmallows and 1 tablespoon of water in a heatproof bowl and heat in the microwave for 30–40 seconds. The marshmallows should melt easily.

2   Gently melt the butter and golden syrup together in a pan on the hob, or in short bursts in the microwave. Gently heat 350g (12oz) of the milk chocolate over a bain-marie or in the microwave and then combine the marshmallows, chocolate, butter and golden syrup and stir together.

3   Mix in the Rice Krispies to thoroughly coat in the mixture. You may need to use gloved hands to totally cover everything.

4   Press the Rice Krispies mixture into the lined tin and push down either with gloved hands or with the back of a spoon. Set aside or chill in the fridge while doing the next steps.

5   Gently heat the Nutella and 100g (3½oz) of the milk chocolate together until melted. Pour over the Rice Krispies mixture. Leave to set in the fridge until the Nutella layer is firm but not solid. Push the Maltesers into the Nutella layer to completely cover the surface.

6   Melt the white chocolate gently in a bain-marie or in the microwave, then stir in the vegetable oil. Make sure the chocolate is cool before pouring it over the Maltesers, ensuring the tops are covered and there is a smooth finish. If you'd like the domed Maltesers showing, use less chocolate!

7   To finish, melt the remaining 30g (1oz) milk chocolate with a dash of vegetable oil and load into a piping bag. Cut the very end off the piping bag and drizzle the chocolate in a circle over the white chocolate layer. Leave for about 5 minutes, then pick up the tin and move it around, allowing the milk chocolate to go in different directions.

8   Leave to set at room temperature or in the fridge before cutting and serving – just watch the sliced Maltesers as they may start to melt if exposed to air for too long.

# GIANT HAZELNUT NUTELLA BALL

Do you ever find yourself sitting there thinking, why don't they make my favourites in giant form?! Whole roasted hazelnuts captured in a Nutella centre, encased by chocolate Nutella ganache, homemade wafer, nibbed hazelnuts and a thick layer of chocolate, this showstopper will be the talk of the party.

## INGREDIENTS

*Serves 20*

**Nutella centre**

40g (1½oz) chopped hazelnuts

4 Ferrero Rocher, chopped

50g (scant ¼ cup) Nutella

**Nutella ganache**

250g (9oz) milk chocolate

100ml (6½ tbsp) double cream

150g (⅔ cup) Nutella

**Wafer**

120g (1 stick) unsalted butter

120g (generous ½ cup) caster sugar

1 egg

40ml (2½ tbsp) full-fat milk

80g (⅔ cup) plain flour

Pinch of salt

OR

400g (14oz) store-bought plain wafers

**Coating**

400g (14oz) milk chocolate

40ml (2½ tbsp) vegetable oil

100g (3½oz) chopped hazelnuts

## SPECIAL EQUIPMENT

Baking tray

23 x 33cm (9 x 13in) baking tray, lined

**1** To make the Nutella centre, preheat the oven to 200°C (180°C fan/400°F/Gas 6). Scatter all the hazelnuts (140g/5oz) over the baking tray and roast for 15 minutes.

**2** Separate the 100g (3½oz) hazelnuts needed for coating, then mix the remaining nuts and Ferrero Rocher for the centre with the Nutella. Heap into a bowl lined with cling film, then chill in the freezer for 10–15 minutes. Once chilled and malleable but not sticky, roll between your hands to form a ball and place in the fridge.

**3** To make the ganache, gently melt the chocolate and cream together over a bain-marie, or in short bursts in the microwave. Add the Nutella and stir until thick and glossy. If the ganache has separated slightly, add a splash more warm double cream and mix. Leave to cool, then chill in the fridge for 1 hour.

**4** Meanwhile, to make the wafer, preheat the oven to 195°C (175°C fan/385°F/Gas 5½).

**5** Cream together the butter and sugar in a bowl. Add the egg and milk and mix. Fold in the flour and salt using a spatula.

**6** Spread the mixture extremely thinly on the lined baking tray. Bake for 15 minutes, or until the edges are golden brown – some areas that are thinner than others may be darker in colour. If the mixture is slightly too thick, there may be a cake-like consistency in some areas, so bake for a few more minutes if necessary. Remove from the oven and leave to cool on the baking tray. Break up into small pieces and place in a bowl. ▶

### Assembling

**7** Remove the ganache from the fridge. Spoon half into a cling film-lined bowl in a heap, making a little well with the back of the spoon in the centre, then place the chilled/frozen Nutella and hazelnut ball on top. Spoon the remaining ganache on top and collect the cling film at the top in order to help form a ball.

**8** Chill in the freezer for 20–30 minutes, or until firmer, then remove from the bowl (but leave the cling film on) and manipulate the ganache between your fingers to form a rounder ball.

**9** Melt the milk chocolate gently on the hob or in short bursts in the microwave, then transfer to a bowl and mix in the oil.

**10** Crush the wafer into smaller and larger pieces, remove the ganache ball from the cling film, then carefully dip the ganache ball into the melted chocolate using gloved hands. Dip the ball in the wafer and roll it around, allowing the wafer to stick to all sides of the ball. Chill for 10 minutes.

**11** Dip the ball in the melted chocolate again (rolling it around as the chocolate catches on the sides), before rolling it in the roasted chopped hazelnuts and any leftover crushed wafer.

**12** Pour the remaining hazelnuts into the leftover melted chocolate and mix in. Set the ball in the fridge for 15 minutes (you can wrap in cling film, if required) before dipping the ball back into the hazelnut-chocolate for its final coat.

**13** Chill in the fridge for several hours, or overnight, until set, then slice and serve.

# RASPBERRY SHORTBREAD SQUARES

A dessert that wouldn't go amiss on Valentine's Day, these pink squares have it all – buttery shortbread flecked with freeze-dried raspberries, a sweet yet tangy raspberry curd and fluffy Italian meringue.

## INGREDIENTS

*Makes 9*

300g (2 sticks plus 4 tbsp) unsalted butter

150g (⅔ cup) caster sugar, plus extra for sprinkling

400g (2¾ cups plus 3 tbsp) plain flour

10g (¼oz) freeze-dried raspberries, plus extra to decorate

**Raspberry curd**

450g (1lb) raspberries, plus extra to decorate

350g (1¾ cups) caster sugar

5 tbsp lemon juice

5 tbsp water

5 egg yolks

10g (2 tsp) cornflour

12g (¼oz) powdered gelatine or 4 leaves of gelatine

150g (1 stick plus 2 tbsp) unsalted butter

**Italian meringue**

2 tbsp water

90g (7½ tbsp) caster sugar

2 egg whites

1 tbsp lemon juice

**Decoration (optional)**

50g (1¾oz) white chocolate, melted and coloured red

## SPECIAL EQUIPMENT

Mixer or hand-held electric whisk
Small heart-shaped cutter

23cm (9in) square tin, lined

Sugar thermometer

Piping bag and nozzle

Kitchen blowtorch

1   To make the shortbread, cream the butter and sugar together in a mixer or using a hand-held electric whisk for a few minutes, then add the flour (change your mixer attachment to the dough hook if using). Beat on a low-medium speed setting until a dough forms.

2   Add the freeze-dried raspberries, making sure to crush some between your fingers to turn to dust. The raspberry dust will give the shortbread a lovely pink colour.

3   Remove the dough from the bowl, separate around 150g (5½oz) and set aside. Wrap the rest in cling film and chill in the fridge for at least 30 minutes. Roll out the remaining dough to about 1cm (½in) thick and cut out nine hearts using the cutter. Place onto the lined baking tray and then chill in the fridge with the rest of the dough. Preheat the oven to 170°C (150°C fan/340°F/ Gas 3½).

4   Roll the chilled 150g (5½oz) dough into a similar-sized shape to your tin, then place it into the lined tin. Use your hands to manipulate the dough into the corners of the tin so that it is evenly distributed and then prick the shortbread with a fork to release the steam while baking.

5   Bake the hearts for 20 minutes and the shortbread tin for 25 minutes, or until the top starts to turn golden. Sprinkle over some caster sugar and leave the shortbread to cool in the tin.

6   To make the raspberry curd, place the raspberries, sugar, lemon juice and water into a saucepan over a medium heat. Simmer for about 10 minutes until the fruit has broken up.

7   Blend the raspberries in a food processor or blender or use the back of a fork to break up any whole fruit remaining. Push the raspberries through a sieve and discard the pulp and seeds.

8   Whisk the egg yolks and cornflour using a hand-held electric whisk, or in a mixer fitted with the whisk attachment, until a paste forms. Continue to whisk as you pour in the hot raspberry liquid. ▶

**9** In a separate bowl, prepare the gelatine. Pour in the gelatine powder or place the gelatine leaves into a cup of about 50ml (3½ tbsp) of cold water. Leave for 5 minutes – the powder will expand, and the leaves will soften.

**10** Return the raspberry mixture to a medium heat and continue to stir until the mixture starts to thicken. Pour in the liquid gelatine and stir or, if using leaves, squeeze out the excess water and add to the mixture. Continue to stir over a medium heat for another few minutes.

**11** Remove from the heat, add the butter and stir until melted. Pour over the shortbread while it's still in the tin and leave to cool before setting in the fridge for 6 hours or overnight. Once ready to serve, remove from the tin and cut into nine portions.

**12** To make the Italian meringue, place the water and sugar in a pan and heat over a low-medium heat until all the sugar has dissolved, making sure to brush any stray sugar down the sides of the pan with a pastry brush.

**13** Whisk together the egg whites and lemon juice in a heatproof bowl for about 2 minutes, or until soft peaks form. Once the sugar syrup reaches 115–120°C (239–248°F) on a sugar thermometer, carefully pour it into the egg white mixture in a continuous stream while still whisking (don't pour the syrup onto the whisk or it may splash back). This will enable all of the egg whites to be evenly cooked before serving.

**14** Continue to whisk until stiffer peaks form. Place into a piping bag with the nozzle of your choice and pipe on top of each shortbread slice. Use a kitchen blowtorch to lightly torch the meringue before decorating with a shortbread heart (we drizzled ours with melted white chocolate coloured red and added more freeze-dried raspberries) and fresh raspberries.

### TOP TIPS

★ Italian meringue can be kept out of the fridge, covered, for a few days, or in the fridge. It may need to be re-whipped. As the meringue is not torched underneath, it may start to slide off the curd after a couple of hours, so we recommend serving immediately.

★ Baking at a lower temperature allows the freeze-dried raspberry pieces to keep their colour in the shortbread.

# COCONUT & RASPBERRY VIENNESE WHIRLS

Soft and delicate shortbread swirl biscuits sandwiched with oozing raspberry jam and sealed together with a coconut kick – there is nothing plain about these XL Viennese Whirls. Prefer traditional? Leave out the coconut and add a little vanilla extract.

## INGREDIENTS

Makes 6

300g (3 sticks plus 4 tbsp) unsalted butter

80g (⅔ cup) icing sugar

5 drops of vanilla extract

275g (2 cups) plain flour

25g (2½ tbsp) cornflour

½ tsp baking powder

### Filling

125g (1 stick) unsalted butter

250g (1¾ cups) icing sugar

5–10 drops of coconut flavouring

About 150g (5½oz) raspberry jam

60g (2¼oz) desiccated coconut

100g (3½oz) white chocolate (optional)

Crushed freeze-dried raspberries

## SPECIAL EQUIPMENT

10cm (4in) cookie cutter

Cake release spray or homemade cake release (page 202 – optional)

Mixer or hand-held electric whisk

Baking trays

Piping bags and open star nozzles

1   Use the cookie cutter to draw six circles onto baking parchment, at least 2.5cm (1in) apart. Turn the paper over and stick down onto a baking tray with butter, cake release spray or homemade cake release. Repeat on another baking tray.

2   In a mixer, beat the butter with the icing sugar for 10 minutes until white and fluffy. Add the vanilla extract and sift in the flour, cornflour and baking powder. Mix on a low-speed setting until just combined.

3   Load the mixture into a piping bag fitted with an open star nozzle. Pipe 12 circles following the cookie cutter guides on the baking trays and chill in the fridge for 30 minutes.

4   Preheat the oven to 180°C (160°C fan/350°F/Gas 4).

5   To make the buttercream, whip the butter until whitened. Sift in the icing sugar and add the coconut flavouring to taste. Combine on a low-speed setting, remembering to scrape down the sides with a spatula.

6   Bake the chilled biscuits for 15 minutes until the edges are golden brown. If the biscuits are too pale, they will fall apart. Leave to cool on the baking trays, then transfer to a wire rack.

7   When cold, use a teaspoon to place about 25g (1oz) of jam in the middle of six of the biscuits (flat-side up), leaving the remaining six plain. Load a piping bag with an open star nozzle and the coconut buttercream. Pipe a circle around the jam and sandwich together with a plain biscuit (placing it flat-side down). Turn the Viennese whirl on its side and sprinkle with desiccated coconut, making sure it sticks to the buttercream. Repeat with the rest. Chill in the fridge for 10 minutes.

8   If using, melt the white chocolate and drizzle over the top of each whirl. Sprinkle some desiccated coconut and crushed freeze-dried raspberries over the white chocolate. Leave to set.

# BUTTERCREAM GRAZING BOARD

Butter boards have become the trend in the charcuterie world, so why not make a sweet version?! The savoury counterpart sees seasoned, softened butter garnished across a board that can then be scooped up with bread, crackers or pretty much anything you might find on a charcuterie board. Choose a couple of recipes from our books to create your own Finch Bakery-inspired buttercream board! Perfect to share during an evening on the sofa – with wine.

## INGREDIENTS

*Serves 2–10 (depending on how much of everything you use)*

School Cake (page 138), No-bake Jammie Dodger Rocky Road (page 147), Raspberry Shortbread Squares (page 165), Breakfast Tarts (page 172) and No-bake Millionaire's Rocky Road (page 151), Raspberry Shortbread Hearts (page 165)

150g (1 stick plus 2 tbsp) unsalted butter

300g (2 cups plus 2 tbsp) icing sugar

1 tsp vanilla extract

Gel or paste food colourings of your choice (to match your theme)

**To serve (suggestions)**

Chocolate fingers

Chocolate-dipped strawberries

Edible flowers

Party rings

Marshmallows

Chocolates

## SPECIAL EQUIPMENT

Mixer or hand-held electric whisk

Piping bags and various nozzles

Cake board or plate (we used a 20cm/8in one)

Ramekins or small serving dishes (optional)

1  Prepare the recipes according to what you'd like your buttercream board to have – we have used recipes in this book (listed opposite), however, you're more than welcome to choose others or serve store-bought items. We have also used chocolate fingers, chocolate-dipped strawberries, edible flowers and party rings to decorate.

2  Cream the butter for 5–10 minutes until whipped, then add the icing sugar and mix. Add the vanilla extract. Split the buttercream into two or three bowls and colour to your desired shades.

3  Load the different colours of buttercream into separate piping bags with different nozzles fitted and pipe decoratively across the cake board or plate. Position some treats on the board on top of the buttercream and leave some in dishes, if you like. Serve immediately before the buttercream crusts over and take lots of photos of your masterpiece before your guests scoop up the buttercream!

### TOP TIPS

★ Try different flavour themes – chocolate buttercream with chocolate brownies and cookies, for example, or different flavours of buttercream like raspberry or lemon.

★ Add spreads in with the buttercream, such as Lotus Biscoff or Nutella, to add extra flavours.

★ Be as experimental as you like – buttercream boards are supposed to look as good as they taste!

# BREAKFAST TARTS

Sweetened pastry encasing a filling of your choice – could breakfast get any better? OK, maybe not part of a well-balanced morning meal and perhaps more suitable for dessert. You can flavour the icing, or leave plain, and decorate with grated chocolate, lemon zest, glacé cherries and flaked almonds.

## INGREDIENTS

*Makes 6*

### Pastry

300g (2½ cups) plain flour

80g (6½ tbsp) granulated sugar

½ tsp salt

250g (2 sticks) cold unsalted butter

1 egg

2 tbsp ice-cold water

### Filling

About 90g (3¼oz) raspberry, strawberry or cherry jam, lemon curd, or spread, such as Nutella or white chocolate hazelnut crème

### Egg wash

1 egg

2 tbsp milk

### Decoration

250g (1¾ cups) icing sugar

Gel food colouring (optional)

Sprinkles of your choice

## SPECIAL EQUIPMENT

Food processor (optional)

Mixer (optional)

Baking tray(s), lined

Pastry brush

1   As the dough needs to be chilled, it can be made in advance. If making by hand (our preferred method), add the dry ingredients to a bowl. Grate in the butter (or add as small cubes) and use your hands to coat the butter with the dry mix. Sift and rub the butter through your fingers until crumbs form. Add the egg and ice-cold water and mix with a spoon until a dough forms. If using a food processor, pulse the flour, sugar and salt together. Cube the cold butter, add, then pulse until breadcrumbs form. Add the egg and ice-cold water and mix until a dough forms.

2   Remove the dough and pat down with some flour if too sticky. Wrap in cling film and chill for 1–2 hours, or longer if possible.

3   Roll out the dough using a rolling pin to about 5mm (¼in) thick. Use a pizza cutter or knife to cut 12 equal-sized rectangles measuring 9 x 13cm (3½ x 5in) – each breakfast tart will use two rectangles. Lay out six of the rectangles on the lined baking tray(s). Spoon 1 heaped tablespoon of filling into the centre of each rectangle.

4   Beat the egg and milk together to make the egg wash and brush around the edge of each filled pastry rectangle using a pastry brush. Cut some slits in the top of the remaining six rectangles to allow the tarts to release steam while baking, then use to top the filled rectangles. Pinch down using your fingers. Use fork prongs to make slits around the edges of each pastry.

5   Chill in the freezer for 20 minutes to ensure the pastry is still cold. Preheat the oven to 200°C (180°C fan/400°F/Gas 6).

6   Brush with more egg wash and bake for 25 minutes, or until golden brown. Leave to cool on the baking tray(s).

7   To make the icing, mix the icing sugar with a small amount of water to your desired consistency, then mix in a few drops of food colouring. When the tarts are cold or just slightly warm, top each with a few spoonfuls of the glacé icing and decorate with some sprinkles. Serve cold or at room temperature.

# CRÈME BRÛLÉE COOKIES

Combining cookies and an elegant French dessert – what could be better?! This recipe uses pastry cream in place of baked custard, but it gives the same delicious flavour with a shorter cooking time. We recommend using bake-stable white chocolate chunks so they keep their shape during baking.

## INGREDIENTS

*Makes 10*

250g (2 sticks) unsalted butter

175g (¾ cup plus 2 tbsp packed) light soft brown sugar

175g (¾ cup plus 2 tbsp) golden caster sugar

1 tsp vanilla extract

3 eggs

2 tsp baking powder

10g (1 tbsp) cornflour

½ tsp salt

½ tsp bicarbonate of soda

650g (5 cups) plain flour

250g (9oz) white chocolate chunks

**Pastry cream**

5 egg yolks

100g (½ cup) granulated sugar, plus extra for topping

30g (3 tbsp) cornflour

500ml (generous 2 cups) full-fat milk

1 tsp vanilla extract

30g (2 tbsp) unsalted butter

## SPECIAL EQUIPMENT

Baking tray, lined

Mixer or hand-held electric whisk

Kitchen blowtorch

1   To make the cookies, cream the butter, both sugars and vanilla extract together, then add the eggs. Sift in the baking powder, cornflour, salt, bicarbonate of soda and flour and mix until a dough forms. Add the chocolate chunks and mix until evenly distributed throughout the dough.

2   Split the dough into ten pieces – each cookie should weigh 150g (5½oz). Roll into balls, flatten slightly and place on the lined tray. Chill for at least 30 minutes – we like to chill for several hours.

3   Preheat the oven to 220°C (200°C fan/425°F/Gas 7). Bake the cookies for 12–14 minutes, or until just browning on top. Leave to cool completely on the baking tray. Chill in the fridge for 1 hour.

4   To make the pastry cream, cream the egg yolks and sugar together with a hand-held electric whisk or in a mixer fitted with the whisk attachment. Add the cornflour and mix again.

5   Heat the milk in a saucepan over a gentle heat until small bubbles start to appear around the sides. Immediately remove from the heat. Slowly pour the milk into the egg mixture while whisking again, this will evenly distribute the warm milk. Return the pan to a medium heat and continuously whisk until thickened – this may take 5–10 minutes. Remove from the heat.

6   Add the vanilla extract and mix, then strain through a sieve to catch any lumps. Add the butter and mix until melted, then place into a bowl and cover with cling film, allowing the plastic to touch the mixture. This will stop a skin from forming. Once cool, place in the fridge for a couple of hours, or until ready to use.

7   Remove the pastry cream from the fridge. Take a large spoonful and place in the middle of each chilled cookie. Use the back of the spoon to spread it around.

8   Sprinkle 1 teaspoon of granulated sugar over the top of each cookie before using the blowtorch to caramelize the sugar, working quickly in circles to evenly distribute the heat. Serve immediately or within an hour or so.

# DELUXE HOT CHOCOLATE WITH TOASTED MARSHMALLOW FLUFF

On a cosy evening watching TV with the family, what could be better for film night than a mug of decadently rich hot chocolate? This marshmallow fluff recipe is one of our absolute favourites, too.

## INGREDIENTS

*Serves 4*

**Homemade marshmallow fluff**

2 tbsp water

50g (¼ cup) caster sugar, plus 1 tbsp

80g (4 tbsp) golden syrup

1 egg white

Dash of lemon juice or ¼ tsp cream of tartar

½ tsp vanilla extract

**Hot chocolate**

700ml (2¾ cups) full-fat milk

60g (5 tbsp) caster sugar

40g (3 tbsp) cocoa powder

200g (7oz) milk chocolate

A few mini marshmallows

## SPECIAL EQUIPMENT

Mixer or hand-held electric whisk

Sugar thermometer

Kitchen blowtorch

1   To make the homemade marshmallow fluff, place the water, 50g (¼ cup) of caster sugar and the golden syrup in a pan and heat over a low-medium heat until all the sugar has dissolved.

2   In a mixer (or using a mixing bowl and a hand-held electric whisk), whisk together the egg white and lemon juice or cream of tartar for a few minutes, or until soft peaks form. Add the tablespoon of caster sugar and continue to whisk until the peaks are glossy and stiff.

3   Once the sugar syrup reaches 115–120°C (239–248°F) on the sugar thermometer, carefully pour it into the egg white mixture in a continuous stream while still whisking (don't pour the syrup onto the whisk or it may splash back). This will enable all of the egg white to be evenly cooked before serving. Add the vanilla extract and continue to whisk on a high speed for 5 minutes.

4   To make the hot chocolate, add the milk, sugar and cocoa powder to a saucepan, whisk together and set over a low-medium heat for 5 minutes, mixing occasionally.

5   Break up the chocolate and stir in, then continue to heat until the chocolate has melted. Keep over a low heat until you are ready to serve. The longer the hot chocolate is heated for, the richer the flavour – 20 minutes was perfect timing for us!

6   To finish, divide the hot chocolate between four mugs or heatproof glasses, top each with a large, heaped dessert-spoonful of marshmallow fluff, sprinkle with a few mini marshmallows and torch lightly with a kitchen blowtorch. Enjoy!

**TOP TIPS ★** The method to make the marshmallow fluff is similar to Italian meringue (see page 165) except it includes golden syrup, which gives a light caramel colour to the fluff. Although we prefer the fluff with the golden syrup, if you'd rather, you can replace it with another 80g (6½ tbsp) of caster sugar. ★ You can also flavour the hot chocolate using a few drops of orange or peppermint oil, if you like.

# NUTELLA FREAKSHAKE

Kids' parties, BBQs, weekend treat; this Nutella milkshake is a simple and fun recipe to follow and is perfect for nearly any occasion!

## INGREDIENTS

Makes 2

170g (¾ cup) Nutella, plus extra, melted, for drizzling

50g (1¾oz) milk chocolate

30g (1oz) hazelnuts, chopped

200ml (scant 1 cup) full-fat milk

6 scoops of vanilla or chocolate ice cream

100ml (6½ tbsp) double cream

**Decoration (per cup)**

Squirty cream

1 Kinder Bueno

1 small Kinder bar

1 Ferrero Rocher

1 Nutella biscuit

Cocoa powder, for dusting

## SPECIAL EQUIPMENT

2 smoothie cups and paper straws

*1* Decorate the smoothie cups by melting 20g (4 tsp) of the Nutella. Use a fork to swirl around the inside of each cup.

*2* Melt the milk chocolate in a microwave or over a bain-marie. Carefully dip the rim of each cup into the chocolate (using a spoon to help) so that 1cm (½in) of the inside of each cup is covered in chocolate. Roll in the hazelnuts or use clean fingers or a spoon to help cover the chocolate completely. Put the cups, rim-side down, on a baking tray and chill until set.

*3* Add the milk, ice cream, remaining 150g (⅔ cup) of Nutella and double cream to a blender and whiz together until liquid.

*4* Fill each chilled cup with milkshake. Use squirty cream to create a whip on top of the shakes and drizzle the extra melted Nutella over the top. Decorate by sticking pieces of Kinder Bueno, Kinder bar and a Ferrero Rocher and Nutella biscuit into the cream and dust with cocoa powder. Add straws and enjoy!

# RASPBERRY & WHITE CHOCOLATE FREAKSHAKE

Follow the instructions above using the following ingredients:

170g (¾ cup) white chocolate spread, plus extra, melted, for drizzling

50g (1¾oz) white chocolate

30g (1oz) freeze-dried raspberry pieces

200ml (scant 1 cup) full-fat milk

6 scoops of raspberry ripple ice cream

100ml (6½ tbsp) double cream

**Decoration (per cup)**

Squirty cream

Mini Jammie Dodgers

White chocolate curls

Glacé cherry

Freeze-dried raspberries

# UNICORN SWISS ROLL

The cutest Swiss roll you've ever seen! Putting your fondant skills to the test, this light and fluffy Swiss roll recipe can be easily adapted to any colour and fillings. Your little ones will love to help decorate this with you and it's the perfect recipe for children's parties.

## INGREDIENTS

*Serves 6–8*

4 eggs

120g (generous ½ cup) caster sugar, plus extra for dusting

Dash of lemon juice

Pinch of salt

120g (scant 1 cup) plain flour

### Filling and decoration

Pink and purple gel food colouring

Yellow (optional) and white fondant icing

Gold lustre spray and edible gold glitter (optional)

175g (1½ sticks) unsalted butter

150g (1¼ cups) icing sugar

Sprinkles of your choice

## SPECIAL EQUIPMENT

Baking tray, lined

Mixer

Piping bags and various nozzles

5cm (2in) deep baking tray or Swiss roll tin about 20 x 30cm (8 x 12in), lined

Angled palette knife

1   First, create the unicorn horn and ears. Preheat the oven to 70°C (50°C fan/160°F/Gas as low as possible). Once the oven has warmed up, turn it off. Take a small amount of yellow fondant icing (pre-made or use a yellow food colouring to colour some white fondant icing) and roll into a thin sausage. Fold in half and, from the join, brush with water and twist together. At the top, use a knife to create a point. Cut to create a proportional-sized horn. To make the ears, roll two balls of white fondant together and press down with your finger. Mould the tops into points. Dye a small amount of fondant pink and add to the inside of the ears. Cut in half to create a flat edge.

2   Put the fondant ears and horn on the lined tray and put into the oven for 3–5 minutes. Leave to cool completely. The fondant should be hard as all the moisture has been removed. To make the horn gold, spray with gold lustre spray and dust with edible gold glitter, if using.

3   Preheat the oven to 200°C (180°C fan/400°F/Gas 6).

4   In the clean metal bowl of a mixer, use the whisk attachment to whisk the eggs and caster sugar together for about 10 minutes until foamy and doubled in size.

5   Add the lemon juice and salt and sift in the flour. Use a spatula to gently fold in the flour, remembering to scrape along the bottom of the bowl to ensure the flour is mixed in.

6   Pour half the batter into a separate bowl, then add pink and purple gel food colourings to each bowl. Carefully fold in the colour, making sure not to overmix and deflate.

7   Load the colours into separate piping bags and alternately pipe lines into the lined tin. Once finished, drop the tin once from a height to knock any large air bubbles out of the batter. Bake for 10–12 minutes, or until the sponge bounces back when pressed.

▶

**8**   Meanwhile, lay out some baking parchment and scatter over some caster sugar. Remove the tin from the oven and carefully turn the sponge out onto the paper. Peel the paper off the bottom of the cake and score a shallow line about 1cm (½in) from the bottom of the cake.

**9**   Use the paper to roll up the hot sponge, using the scored line to start as a guide. Remember to put the seam side down and leave to cool completely on a wire rack.

**10**   Make a batch of **VANILLA BUTTERCREAM**, following the recipe on page 200, using the quantities listed on page 180. Once the sponge has cooled, unroll it and use an angled palette knife to evenly spread over the buttercream, leaving enough to pipe a "mane" on top. Carefully roll the sponge back up and put in the fridge for 15 minutes to set.

**11**   Colour the remaining buttercream pink and purple and load into two separate piping bags with different nozzle tips. Pipe a "mane" in rosettes and drop stars along the middle of the roll and use sprinkles to decorate. Arrange the fondant icing horn and ears at the front.

**TOP TIPS**

★ If you aren't confident using fondant icing, there are lots of chocolate moulds available to create a horn and ears for your unicorn – both methods can be made in advance.

★ The Swiss roll can be made with multiple colours, just beware of overmixing the batter.

★ Some people use a thin tea towel to roll up the sponge instead of baking parchment – if you prefer this method, make sure not to wash it in anything scented before using.

*Makes 6*

**Chocolate fudge cake**

70g (5 tbsp) unsalted butter

70ml (4½ tbsp) vegetable oil

3 eggs

10–12 drops of orange extract

135g (⅔ cup packed) light soft brown sugar

100g (½ cup) caster sugar

200ml (scant 1 cup) boiling water

½ tsp fine instant coffee

½ tsp salt

50g (½ cup) cocoa powder

170g (1⅓ cups) plain flour

¼ tsp bicarbonate of soda

1 tsp baking powder

**Decoration**

50ml (scant ¼ cup) double cream

100g (3½oz) milk chocolate

100g (6½ tbsp) unsalted butter

20g (¼ cup) cocoa powder

180g (1⅓ cups) icing sugar

600g (1lb 5oz) Maltesers

100g (3½oz) white chocolate

Green and red fondant icing

Edible gold or silver glitter spray

## SPECIAL EQUIPMENT

Mixer

Cake release spray or homemade cake release (see page 202) (optional)

6 large suet pudding tins

Baking tray

Piping bags

Holly leaf cutter/stamp

6 x thick 12cm (4½in) silver cake cards (optional)

# INDIVIDUAL MALTESER CHRISTMAS PUDDINGS

**The perfect decadent place setting dessert for any Christmas table. Wow your family with our individual fudge cake puddings, filled with chocolate ganache, encased in Maltesers and topped with edible holly and berries.**

*1* Preheat the oven to 180°C (160°C fan/350°F/Gas 4).

*2* Melt the butter in the microwave or in a pan on the hob over a low heat.

*3* In the mixer bowl, add the vegetable oil, eggs, orange extract, light brown sugar, caster sugar and melted butter. Mix on a high-speed setting for 5 minutes.

*4* In another bowl, add the boiling water to the coffee, salt and cocoa powder and mix until liquid. Pour into the butter/sugar mixture and combine.

*5* In a third bowl, sift the flour, bicarbonate of soda and baking powder together. Slowly spoon the dry ingredients into the wet and use a spatula to combine. Do not overmix.

*6* Sieve the entire batter to get rid of any lumps.

*7* Use cake release spray or homemade cake release to coat the insides of the suet pudding tins and place on a baking tray. Fill each tin three-quarters full.

*8* Bake (on the baking tray) for 25–30 minutes, or until a cocktail stick inserted into the centre comes out clean. Leave to cool in the pudding tins for 5 minutes, then turn out onto a wire rack, bottom down, and leave to cool completely. ▶

### Decoration

**9** Prepare a ganache by heating the double cream and then adding the milk chocolate. Stir until thickened.

**10** Whip the butter until whitened, then add the cocoa powder and icing sugar, mixing on a low-speed setting. Wipe down the sides of the bowl and mix slowly again. Load a piping bag with the buttercream and set aside.

**11** Turn the sponges over and use the handle end of a teaspoon to create a small round hole in the middle of each, by twisting it around. Load a piping bag with the ganache and, either using a round nozzle or a snipped piping bag, fill the holes. Chill for 10 minutes, or until the ganache has solidified.

**12** Use the bag of buttercream to blob onto the cake cards, and stick the sponges, bottom down. Squeeze some more chocolate buttercream onto the top of each sponge and, using an angled spatula, spread the buttercream around the sponge, covering it completely.

**13** Line up Maltesers around the base of each sponge, pushing them into the buttercream. Cover each whole sponge with Maltesers until all six are covered. Chill in the fridge for 10–15 minutes.

**14** Meanwhile, temper the white chocolate (see page 216) and cut out twelve green holly leaves from the green fondant icing using the holly leaf cutter/stamp. Use the palms of your hands to create small balls for the berries from the red fondant icing.

**15** Remove the puddings from the fridge and carefully spoon over the tempered white chocolate, letting it partially run down the sides of each. Leave until tacky and then stick on the holly leaves. Use a dab of water on a clean finger to wet the holly leaves and arrange three balls of red fondant for the berries on each. Spray with edible glitter. Serve.

**16** If gift wrapping, take a square of cellophane and place a pudding on a cake card in the centre. Grab all four corners of the cellophane and pull up above the Christmas pudding and secure with ribbon. Cut off any excess cellophane. Repeat for the remaining puddings.

# BROWNIE YULE LOG

This makes an extremely fudgy brownie – the method entails baking the brownie and then using it to form a dough, before rolling it up and encasing it in chocolate. We recommend preparing it up to a week in advance and storing in the fridge until needed.

## INGREDIENTS

*Serves 10–12*

3 eggs

280g (1½ cups minus 1½ tbsp) caster sugar

150g (5½oz) milk or dark chocolate

270g (2 sticks plus 2 tbsp) unsalted butter

100g (1 cup) cocoa powder

120g (scant 1 cup) plain flour

### Filling

150g (5½oz) spread of your choice, such as milk chocolate spread, Nutella or Lotus Biscoff

50g (1¾oz) milk, dark or white chocolate

### Decoration

200g (7oz) milk or dark chocolate

Dash of vegetable oil

Icing sugar (optional)

Fresh fruit, such as raspberries and figs, halved

## SPECIAL EQUIPMENT

Mixer (preferably) or a hand-held electric whisk

23cm (9in) square tin or 20 x 30cm (8 x 12in) rectangular tin or 20cm (8in) round cake tin, lined

23 x 33cm (9 x 13in) baking tin or tray

Holly leaf cutter/stamp (optional)

*1* Preheat the oven to 180°C (160°C fan/350°F/Gas 4).

*2* Whisk the eggs and caster sugar together for a minute or two using a mixer on a medium speed setting or a hand-held electric whisk.

*3* Place the chocolate and butter in a bowl or saucepan and gently heat together in the microwave or on the hob. Once melted, mix until the butter and chocolate are completely combined. Slowly pour the melted butter/chocolate mixture into the whisked eggs and combine on a low-speed setting.

*4* Sift the cocoa powder and plain flour into the bowl and mix in using a spatula. The brownie batter should be smooth and glossy.

*5* Pour the batter into the lined tin and bake for 25 minutes. Remove from the oven and leave in the tin to cool completely. Then chill the tin in the fridge for a couple of hours.

*6* Cut the chilled brownie into small pieces and place in the bowl of a mixer. Turn on the mixer and allow a dough to form. (Alternatively, beat with a hand-held electric whisk, however, the brownie dough may be more resistant to a whisk compared to a mixer.)

*7* Take the brownie dough out of the bowl and set aside. Line the baking tin/tray cling film and use a rolling pin or your fists and fingers to spread the brownie dough out to fill the tin. The dough should be evenly spread, however on one side of the tin (a 25cm/10in edge), allow about 2.5cm (1in) of dough to be manipulated thinner – just use your thumb to press down. This will help with the rolling process.

*8* Chill in the fridge for 10 minutes or until the dough has firmed slightly. Melt your filling spread of choice in a microwave-proof bowl for 10 or so seconds, then add the chocolate and heat again. Mix together until completely melted. This will allow the filling to set slightly firmer than just using the spread on its own.

▶

**9** Remove the tray from the fridge and spread the filling across the dough, leaving a border of a few centimetres on each side of the long sides of the tin and at the thicker edge of the short side. This is to ensure no filling spills out while rolling.

**10** Place the tray back into the fridge and keep checking on the filling's consistency; the filling needs to have firmed slightly, but still be soft enough so it is easy to roll. The tray should remain in the fridge for no longer than 5–10 minutes; if the filling has totally firmed up it will crack.

**11** Take the tray out of the fridge and remove the brownie from the tin/tray; simply pull up the cling film and lay on a work surface. Working from the thin side, start to manipulate the brownie dough into a small roll. The cling film can be removed; however, it may also be used as a tool to help achieve a tighter roll. Let the dough roll between your fingers until the entire length of brownie dough has been rolled up, pulling off the cling film if you have decided to keep it on. If the brownie dough starts to crack, it has been refrigerated for too long and it should be left out until it has warmed slightly. If there are only small cracks, the warmth of your fingers should be able to blend them back together. If the roll does not easily roll, or the filling starts to crack, leave the tray out while it comes back closer to room temperature. If the rolling is awkward but does not crack, the filling may be too firm and will show quite angularly within the Yule log and there may be some gaps. The dough and filling need to be at the perfect temperature to enable the perfect roll.

**12** Once the brownie Yule log has been rolled, use your fingers to smooth down the seam of the log. Wrap tightly in cling film and store in the fridge for several hours until firm.

### Decoration

**13** Once firmed in the fridge, heat the milk or dark chocolate gently in the microwave or in a pan on the hob until melted. If you would like an easier cut, add a little vegetable oil to the chocolate. If the oil is not added, the chocolate can crack once cutting the slices, and this may not be the effect you are trying to achieve.

**14** Place some melted chocolate on a piece of baking parchment and place the chilled log on top. Pour the rest of the chocolate over the top of the log and allow it to run down the sides; use a palette knife to ensure the chocolate coats the sides of the log and the ends.

**15** Using the palette knife, run the edge down the length of the roll to make ridges to replicate the tree bark, working quickly as the chocolate will soon set against the cold brownie.

**16** Scrape any excess melted chocolate that may have pooled at the bottom of the log and then leave it to set. Pull the baking parchment from the bottom of the log and carefully remove any excess chocolate using a sharp knife. You can also use a sharp knife to create grooves replicating tree bark and rings on each end.

**17** Once set and on the day of serving, it's time to decorate! Top with fresh fruit and dust with icing sugar, if you like.

**18** Store in the fridge until needed. Fix on the fondant decorations, then dust with icing sugar or spray with edible glitter once the log is out of the fridge and just before cutting.

### TOP TIPS

★ White chocolate or ganache can be used to replace milk or dark chocolate for the coating for a non-traditional decoration.

★ We recommend pairing milk chocolate with fillings such as milk chocolate spread or Nutella, and white chocolate with white chocolate hazelnut crème, white chocolate spread or caramel.

★ For a milk chocolate ganache, heat 75ml (⅓ cup) double cream with 150g (5½oz) milk chocolate and mix until combined. Leave to cool and then spread along the log – the texture is gloopier than melted chocolate – using a palette knife to make imprints like bark. The ganache coating should stay glossy and be easy to cut, however, if you'd still like a chocolate ganache coating but the ganache to be firmer, whisk the cooled ganache with a mixer or hand-held electric whisk. Whipped chocolate ganache sets very fast, so work quickly!

★ Experiment with thinner layers by splitting the dough in half and then layering the brownie layers with two layers of filling before rolling up. It will be slightly trickier to ensure both layers of dough roll consistently with each other, however, the effect of more rings once cut is striking.

★ If you would like to use another brownie recipe, there is a possibility that your mixer or hand-held electric whisk will not be able to break up the baked brownie easily. As there may be more "crust" on top of the used above, once mixed, it may appear crumbly compared to the brownie above. Adding a few spoonfuls of buttercream into the mixer will help bind the dough together to a more velvety texture (similar to the recipe here).

# SUMMER FRUITS CHEESECAKE BROWNIE ROLL

When Christmas is over but you're still itching to make a fabulous non-festive brownie roll, what can you do? Thankfully this recipe is versatile enough that it's not just for Christmas. You could make it into a replica of that famous caterpillar cake, theme it around Halloween (orange, purple or green swirl anyone?), or add different fillings depending on the season.

## INGREDIENTS

*Serves 10–12*

3 eggs

280g (1½ cups minus 1½ tbsp) caster sugar

150g (5½oz) milk or dark chocolate

270g (2 sticks plus 2 tbsp) unsalted butter

100g (1 cup) cocoa powder

120g (scant 1 cup) plain flour

**Cheesecake filling**

150g (5½oz) white chocolate

340g (11½oz) full-fat cream cheese

65g (½ cup) icing sugar

A dash of lemon juice

Vanilla extract, to taste

200ml (scant 1 cup) double cream

**Decoration**

300–350g (10–12oz) white chocolate

Fresh fruit – we like strawberries, blueberries, raspberries, blackberries and cherries

Icing sugar, for dusting

## SPECIAL EQUIPMENT

Mixer (preferably) or a hand-held electric whisk

23cm (9in) square tin or 20 x 30cm (12 x 8in) rectangular tin or 20cm (8in) round cake tin, lined

23 x 33cm (9 x 13in) baking tin or tray

*1* Make the **BROWNIE YULE LOG** using the quantities listed here and following the method on page 187.

*2* To make the cheesecake filling, melt the white chocolate in a bain-marie, or in short bursts in the microwave, and leave to cool. Whisk together the cream cheese, icing sugar, dash of lemon juice and vanilla extract in a bowl for 1 minute, or until smooth and slightly thickened. Add the melted chocolate and mix in.

*3* In a separate bowl, whip the double cream until stiff but not hard. Gently fold the cream through the cream cheese mixture using a spatula, then chill in the fridge for 30 minutes to set.

*4* Use a palette knife to evenly distribute the cheesecake filling across the brownie roll, leaving any excess in the bowl to serve alongside.

*5* Use the same rolling technique as on page 188, making sure you are extra gentle due to the creamy consistency of a no-bake cheesecake filling. This roll will likely end up half brownie, half cheesecake. Leave in the fridge overnight to set.

*6* The next day, decorate the roll with the melted white chocolate following the method on pages 188 and 189. Top with the fresh fruit and a dusting of icing sugar. Store in the fridge until needed. Eat within 5 days and enjoy!

**TOP TIP ★** We have found rolling the brownie roll while still in the cling film reduces the chances of cracking – we position the baking tin/tray on the work surface and push it up against a wall. Then, after using your fingers to create the initial roll, pull the cling film forwards tightly, using the force of the baking tin/tray against the wall to help keep the roll tight.

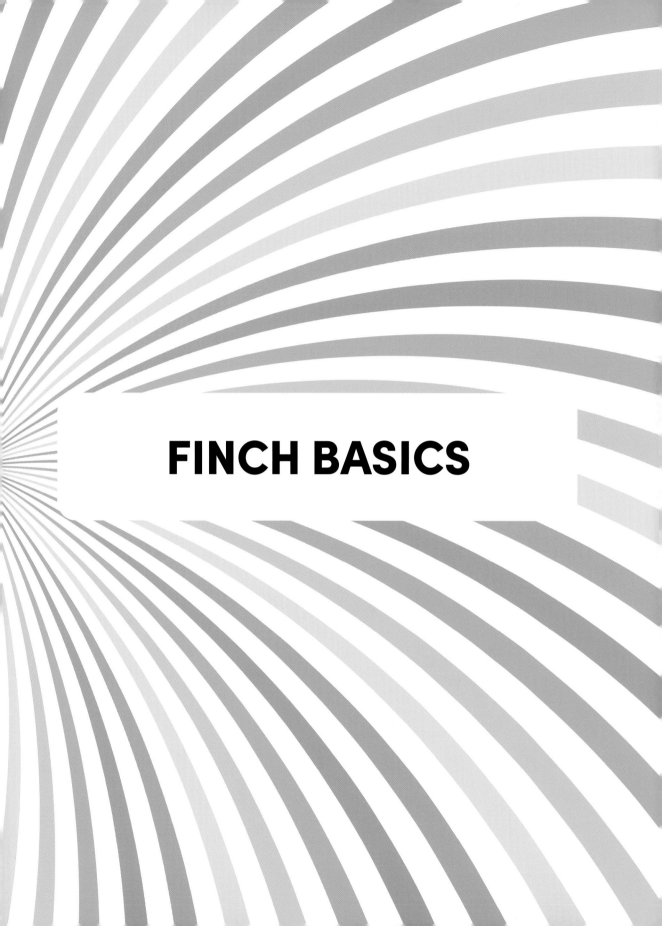

# FINCH BASICS

# EQUIPMENT

From essential tools that you may already have at home to specialist baking equipment that can help to give your cakes a professional finish, here is the equipment we couldn't do without.

## MIXER / HAND-HELD ELECTRIC WHISK

Most recipes in this book call for a mixer. We use a KitchenAid, however, there are so many other brilliant mixers available to choose from as well. If you don't have a mixer, you can use a hand-held electric whisk instead.

## CAKE & BAKING TINS

Most recipes in this book use either a 20cm (8in) round, or a 20 x 30cm (8 x 12in) rectangular or a 23cm (9in) square tin. We recommend rectangular and square tins that have straight sides (rather than tapered sides) to ensure even bakes. We use Silverwood cake tins.

## CAKE DRUMS

We prefer to use cake drums, which are slightly thicker than cake boards, to create a stable base for all of our celebration cakes. A cake drum should be at least 7.5cm (3in) wider than the un-iced cake to accommodate the crumb coat, buttercream layer and a decorative border around the base of the cake, if required.

## WEIGHING SCALES

Combining baking ingredients can be an exact science, which is why recipes call for accurate measurements – it's best to use electric scales.

## ANGLED PALETTE KNIFE

You can use this versatile tool to apply, smooth and make patterns in buttercream, lift cookies from baking trays, spread batter, or apply gel food colouring, among many things.

## CAKE SCRAPERS

We use our own range of metal cake scrapers, but there are plenty of metal, acrylic and plastic versions available. Essential for achieving a smooth finish or adding patterns such as stripes or a zigzag to buttercream, a cake scraper is a must-have for impressive cake decoration.

## PIPING BAGS AND NOZZLES

Good-quality piping bags are vital for successful piping – we recommend large, anti-slip eco or biodegradable plastic piping bags. Owning every single nozzle is not imperative; start off with a couple of open and closed star nozzles and build your collection as your skills grow.

## PASTRY BRUSH

We use a pastry brush (or a paintbrush) to wash the sugar off the sides of a pan to prevent it from burning, to create chocolate brush strokes, to apply cake release to tins and to apply gold or silver leaf to decorate the side of cakes.

## SUGAR THERMOMETER

A few recipes in this book call for a sugar thermometer to ensure the correct temperature is met. This is for several different reasons including killing bacteria, tempering chocolate and ensuring sugar will take on its correct form.

## SPIRIT LEVEL

Yes, you read that correctly; we used to use a (clean!) spirit level after trimming the top of a sponge to ensure all of the layers were level. These days we have invested in an expensive cake leveller called Agbay, which saves time and ensures perfectly level cakes every time.

## TURNTABLE

A good turntable ensures buttercream goes on evenly and prevents constantly having to move the cake. We recommend a heavy-duty metal one rather than plastic, to ensure the weight of the cake is supported and the turntable rotates smoothly to make decorating so much easier.

## DOWELS

Cake dowels are wooden or plastic straws or sticks. They are pushed into a cake to add stability to it, and are essential for tiered cakes to make sure the layers don't move or collapse.

# INGREDIENTS

**Most ingredients in this book can be bought from supermarkets, excluding some specialist items such as bake-stable chocolate chunks, certain types of spreads, chocolate and specialist flavourings. Here are a few things to note regarding the ingredients we use.**

## EGGS

All of our recipes use UK medium (US large) free-range eggs.

## BUTTER

Unless specified otherwise, butter should be softened and at room temperature before using.

## FOOD COLOURINGS

There are many brands out there, but we mainly use Wilton, Sugarflair and Colour Mill.

## WHITENERS

There are lots of icing and buttercream whiteners on the market, including white colouring gels and whitening powders. We use whitening powder to create a super white buttercream. If you do not have any whitener, we recommend whipping the butter for 5–10 minutes before adding the icing sugar. You can also add a pin prick amount of purple food colouring to counteract the yellow.

## DECORATIONS

Most quality decorations such as sprinkles, lustre dusts, gold and silver leaf, and gel or oil-based food colourings are available to purchase from specialist baking shops or online.

# COLOURINGS

**There are a variety of different products on the market, and each one can affect the taste or texture of whatever you are colouring.**

### OIL-BASED

Oil-based food colouring has been developed specifically with chocolate in mind. It contains soya lecithin, which acts as an emulsifier between water and chocolate so that it maintains its fluidity. Oil-based colourings can be used for buttercream and sponges. *Our favourite for: Drips (see pages 214–215); White Chocolate Ganache (see page 201). Recommended brands: Colour Mill; Wilton.*

### POWDER

Powdered colours are mostly available online and they are great for recipes that call for no extra water. Add a little bit to alcohol or lemon juice to use as an edible paint, or add a small amount at a time to a wet mixture and stir in until fully incorporated. *Our favourite for: painting chocolate drips.*

### PASTE

The colour in these is highly pigmented so a little goes a long way – a tiny dab on the end of a cocktail stick is enough! It is best to build up the shade bit by bit. Sometimes streaks of paste can catch and cause inconsistencies in the colour. Nonetheless, it is worth making the investment in some high-quality colourings that will keep in your baking cupboard for ages! *Our favourite for: Buttercream (see page 200); fondant. Recommended brand: Sugarflair.*

### GEL

Colouring gels are probably the most versatile product on the market. Gel is similar to paste – slightly less concentrated in colour but still gives really vibrant shades while keeping the consistency of your baking mix. Some brands are available in supermarkets, however, we have found these are not as pigmented as those you can buy online. *Our favourite for: Buttercream (see page 200); sponges; fondant. Recommended brands: Wilton; Magic Colours; Pro Gel.*

### NATURAL

Food colourings from natural sources are ideal if you would like to use less synthetic products or if you are baking for people with particular nutritional requirements. Generally, the colourants are derived from plants, such as beetroot, peppers or turmeric, and you only require a small amount of product. They may affect taste if used straight from the natural source and if using a liquid natural food colouring, the colours may not be as vibrant as when using synthetic colours. *Recommended brands/products: PME natural food colouring; beetroot; paprika; turmeric.*

# FLAVOURINGS

Extracts and essences are both used to flavour foods, but differ greatly. They are a brilliant way of achieving flavours that would be unobtainable naturally – think candy floss and bubblegum!

## VANILLA EXTRACT & ESSENCE

Vanilla extract – generally preferred in baking due to taste and quality – is made from real vanilla beans and is therefore more expensive than essence, which contains synthetic vanilla flavouring. Imitation vanilla is best avoided due to its synthetic taste.

## HIGH-STRENGTH FLAVOURINGS

Liquid flavours are amazing for offering variety throughout your bakes. Even natural flavours such as orange and lemon juice are available in oil form; real lemon juice is quite sharp, while oils tend to be sweeter. Flavours such as lemon, orange, peppermint and almond are readily available in most supermarkets and are brilliant for flavouring buttercream.

A high-strength flavouring is particularly useful if you are making a larger batch of sponges or something that cannot tolerate extra water in the recipe. There are different concentrations of flavourings available on the market, with supermarket brands tending to be weaker and needing more product for an intense flavour. *Recommended brand: Foodie Flavours.*

# SPRINKLES

Sprinkles have come a long way since the "hundreds and thousands" days. Now available in every colour and shape, sprinkles are our favourite decoration and we use any excuse to throw them on (and in!) our bakes.

## BAKE-STABLE SPRINKLES

As sprinkles are just small pieces of sugar, they can easily melt, so sprinkles that are bake-stable are imperative when exposing them to high temperatures. These are available on specialist websites. *Recommended brands: Shire Bakery; Super Streusel.*

## GOLD & SILVER LEAF / EDIBLE GLITTER

Steer clear of metallic leaf and glitter that is deemed "non toxic" but not edible – these products should not be consumed and are for decoration purposes only. Genuine gold and silver leaf is expensive! Carefully apply loose gold or silver leaf with a dry paintbrush to your bakes. Try not to use your fingers as it will stick to you and most of the product will be lost. Spray edible glitter at a distance from your cake and watch your masterpiece sparkle! There are a range of colours and styles to choose from. *Recommended brand: Barnabas Blattgold.*

# BUTTERCREAM

One of the most important parts of cake decoration is getting the correct consistency for buttercream. If it is too wet, it won't hold its shape and can melt off the cake; if it's too stiff, you may find it difficult to squeeze through the piping bag. The trick is to soften the butter enough at the start to end up with a silky mixture. It is best made right before you are going to use it, but if you make it in advance and store it in the fridge, you can loosen it up with a splash of warm water or milk and bring it up to room temperature before using. For best results, mix buttercream using a mixer or hand-held electric whisk.

## PLAIN BUTTERCREAM

250g (2 sticks) unsalted butter, softened
500g (3½ cups) icing sugar, plus extra if needed

Add the butter to the bowl of a mixer and whip on a high speed for 5 minutes – this may take a little longer if using a hand-held electric whisk. Scrape down the sides of the bowl with a spatula and whip for another 30 seconds. This will turn the butter more white than yellow.

Sift the icing sugar into the bowl and combine on a medium setting, remembering to stop and scrape around the sides to mix in everything fully.

## FLAVOURED BUTTERCREAM

250g (2 sticks) unsalted butter, softened
500g (3½ cups) icing sugar, plus extra if needed
Extract of your choice, to taste (almond, peppermint, caramel, candy floss... the list is endless!)

Follow the **PLAIN BUTTERCREAM** method (see above), adding your extract or flavouring of choice. The strength, brand and type of flavouring will determine how much you need – when it comes to extracts, add a little at a time until you reach the required strength of flavour.

## VANILLA BUTTERCREAM

250g (2 sticks) unsalted butter, softened
500g (3½ cups) icing sugar, plus extra if needed
1 tsp vanilla extract or vanilla bean paste

Follow the **PLAIN BUTTERCREAM** method (see left). Add the vanilla extract or paste and mix for a further 15 seconds. You can add more extract or paste if you want more flavour.

## CHOCOLATE BUTTERCREAM

250g (2 sticks) unsalted butter, softened
500g (3½ cups) icing sugar, plus extra if needed
100g (1 cup) cocoa powder

Follow the **PLAIN BUTTERCREAM** method (see left), but sift in the cocoa powder with the icing sugar. For a darker colour, replace some of the icing sugar with extra cocoa powder.

### TOP TIPS

★ If the consistency of the buttercream is too wet, sift in an extra 50g (⅓ cup) of icing sugar at a time until it has stiffened up, or chill it in the fridge for a short while.

★ A dairy-free alternative for unsalted butter is baking block. Some brands are vegan but they can taste less buttery. Be mindful that using baking block for buttercream in celebration cakes can cause the cake to start melting much faster than real butter, which may compromise its stability and structure.

# CHOCOLATE GANACHE

You can use chocolate ganache as a filling alongside buttercream to create an even richer, fudgier flavour in your cakes. It's also perfect for sandwiching between cookies and for filling cookie cups and tempered chocolate shells – try not to finish it off by the spoonful before getting around to adding it to your bakes!

## MILK OR DARK CHOCOLATE GANACHE

300ml (1¼ cups) double cream, plus extra if needed
600g (1lb 5oz) milk or dark chocolate, chopped
Special equipment: Mixer or hand-held electric whisk

Heat the cream in a small saucepan over a low heat until it steams and just starts to bubble. Put the chopped chocolate in a heatproof bowl and pour the hot cream over. Leave the chocolate to melt and gently stir to combine.

Alternatively, put the chocolate and cream in a microwave-proof bowl and heat in 30-second intervals at full power until the chocolate has melted. Use a wooden spoon to mix the chocolate and the cream together.

Ganache should have a thick, silky consistency and can be kept at room temperature for up to 2 days or stored in the fridge for up to 1 month.

To whip it, bring it to room temperature and use the whisk attachment of a mixer (or a hand-held electric whisk) to whip for several minutes until loose and creamy. If the ganache is too stiff, whip in a splash of extra cream or milk, a little at a time. If the ganache is too runny, put it back in the fridge for a while before you whip it again.

## WHITE CHOCOLATE GANACHE

200ml (scant 1 cup) double cream, plus extra if needed
600g (1lb 5oz) white chocolate, chopped
Special equipment: Mixer or hand-held electric whisk

Follow the method for **MILK OR DARK CHOCOLATE GANACHE** (see left), replacing the milk or dark chocolate with white chocolate and using slightly less double cream – the milk and dark chocolate ganache uses a ratio of 2:1 chocolate to cream, whereas white chocolate ganache uses a ratio of 3:1 chocolate to cream.

# LINING TINS

Lining tins with baking parchment is an essential step when preparing your baked goods. Using baking parchment achieves high-quality bakes with even sides.

## HOMEMADE CAKE RELEASE

*Makes 330g (11½oz) or about 1 jam jar*

110g (½ cup) vegetable shortening
110g (½ cup) vegetable oil
110g (scant 1 cup) plain flour

If you've ever struggled getting your cakes out of obscure-shaped tins, and greasing with butter just doesn't work, this is the quick and simple recipe for you. Cakes will slide right out of the tins after using this method:

Soften the vegetable shortening and whip in a mixer until creamed. Add the oil and mix again. Sift in the flour and whip on high until it is very smooth and white in colour.

To use, paint generously into cake and cupcake tins with a pastry brush before adding batter and baking as usual. Store in an airtight container in the fridge for up to a year. Soften in the microwave at full power before using.

## LINING A SQUARE BAKING TIN

Lay out the baking parchment and place the square or rectangular tin on top with space all around. Draw around the base of the tin with a pencil. Measure the depth of the tin and add it on around the whole square or rectangle.

Cut a strip of parchment slightly longer than the length of the long side of the tin. Grease the entire tin with butter or oil and stick the strip to the tin, overlapping the corners. From both edges on the long side of the larger piece of parchment, make two vertical cuts where the

original base is drawn onto the baking parchment. Slide the uncut edge up to the strip, then gently ease the parchment into the tin and up the sides. When the base is in place, ease the cut flaps inwards and stick down with a little more butter or oil.

## LINING A ROUND BAKING TIN

If you are lining one tin, place the base of the tin directly onto the baking parchment and draw around the edge with a pencil. Cut the circle out neatly with a pair of scissors. If you are lining multiples of the same tin, fold the parchment over as many times as tins you have and then draw around the base. Cut the layered parchment neatly following the guide of the circle to achieve several perfectly cut circles.

Cut long strips of baking parchment, a little thicker than the depth of the tin, and fold the parchment 2.5cm (1in) up from the bottom. Use the scissors to snip upwards towards the fold, leaving around 2.5cm (1in) in between each snip.

Grease the tin using either butter or oil and stick the long strip around the sides of the tin, angling it down. Make sure the pieces you have snipped lay flat around the bottom of the tin.

Place the circle of parchment into the bottom of the tin over the top of the flat pieces.

## LINING A BAKING TRAY

Baking trays covered in baking parchment are perfect for baking cookies of all shapes and sizes. The parchment helps reduce hot and cool spots within the oven, reduces spreading and, of course, prevents anything sticking to the tray, creating an evenly baked cookie. It's as simple as drawing around your baking tray directly onto the baking parchment, cutting it out and securing it down with a little butter or oil onto the tray.

# PIPING BAGS & NOZZLES

## NOZZLES & COUPLERS

At Finch Bakery we use our own branded nozzles, which are named after our amazing team members at Finch Bakery! However, thereare plenty of other brands around and they all offer similar styles and sizes.

A coupler is a two-part plastic device that unscrews, allowing a piping nozzle to drop through it and it is then secured to the piping bag when screwed back together. This allows you to change the nozzle without changing the piping bag. A nozzle can be used inside a piping bag with or without a coupler.

## PIPING BAGS

There are a variety of different piping bags on the market. Due to ease and hygiene purposes, we use eco-plastic piping bags, however, you may prefer to use washable piping bags that can be reused.

## LOADING A PIPING BAG

Place the piping bag in a tall jug or glass with the nozzle pointing downwards, and then roll the piping bag over the sides of the container to expose the nozzle inside. Half-fill the bag – do not add more than this or it will be too hard to pipe or the bag may split under the pressure. Unfold the sides of the piping bag and twist at the top so that the buttercream stays inside the bag. Snip off the end of the piping bag when you're ready to start piping.

## HOLDING A PIPING BAG

Holding a piping bag works differently for everyone, just like holding a pencil! One method is to grip the top of the bag from above and clench your fingers and thumb around the bag. Then use your other hand to pincer your forefinger and thumb around the base of the piping bag (near the nozzle) to assist the dominant hand squeezing out the buttercream. However you do it, hold the piping bag vertically initially, and squeeze to get rid of any excess air and buttercream to prevent spluttering.

## MULTI-TONE PIPING

Mixing colours together in a piping bag works well for the first few uses before the colours begin to blend together. Follow these steps to achieve clean colours with multi-tone piping:

For precise lines, put each of your different colours of buttercream into separate piping bags and cut the ends off, ready to pipe.

Place a piece of cling film on a flat work surface and pipe fairly thick lines of each colour directly next to each other in the middle of the cling film. The lines should be a bit shorter than the length of the piping bag. You can also pipe another layer of lines on top, if required.

Carefully roll the cling film into a sausage-shape, keeping the lines intact, and secure each side with a twist. Cut off one of the ends and insert into a piping bag fitted with the desired nozzle.

Pipe as desired and once the buttercream has run out; simply remove the empty cling film and replace with a fresh batch.

# PIPING TECHNIQUES

From beautifully piped roses to simple swirls, no matter how they are decorated, cupcakes are still a bestseller in our shops! New piping techniques and nozzles of all shapes and sizes keep celebration cakes and cupcakes on-trend. Good equipment makes all the difference when piping and decorating to ensure a professional-looking result. These piping techniques can also be used on your sheet cakes and tray bakes to create wonderful effects.

### CLASSIC ROSETTE

*Favourite nozzles: large star nozzle; open star nozzle*

Point the piping bag vertically and, starting in the centre, touch the cupcake with the nozzle. Applying medium pressure, squeeze the piping bag and allow the buttercream to slowly swirl outwards until you reach the edge of the cupcake, and then squeeze and gently pull away to finish.

### CLASSIC SWIRL

*Favourite nozzles: open star nozzle; closed star nozzle*

Point the piping bag vertically and, starting at the edge of the cupcake, touch the cupcake with the nozzle. Applying medium pressure, squeeze the piping bag and allow the buttercream to slowly swirl around the edge of the cupcake, working inwards, until you have covered the sponge. Gently squeeze the piping bag and lift away from the cupcake to finish with a small whip on top.

## SHELLS

*Favourite nozzles: open star nozzle; closed star nozzle; drop star nozzle*

Point the piping bag at a 45° angle and touch the sponge at your starting point. Squeeze firmly and allow the shell shape to form, curling upwards before lowering the nozzle downwards. Quickly release and gently pull away. The next shell will cover the last shell's tail. Repeat in a pattern, or around the edge of a cake.

## OPEN STAR

*Favourite nozzles: open star nozzle; drop star nozzle*

Point the piping bag vertically and touch the cupcake with the nozzle at your starting position. Squeeze gently so that a small star shape appears and then lift the piping bag away from the cupcake; repeat accordingly.

## RUFFLES

*Favourite nozzles: flat ribbon nozzle; petal nozzle*

Hold the piping bag on its side and make sure the widest part of the triangular nozzle is against the cake and the thinnest part is at the top. Squeeze with medium-firm pressure and the buttercream will come out in a line standing up. Gently zigzag your hand while maintaining the same pressure, then release the pressure and grip to tail the ruffle off.

## RUFFLE ROPE

*Favourite nozzles: open star nozzle; large star nozzle; drop star nozzle*

Hold the piping bag on its side at your starting point and squeeze with medium-firm pressure to form a thick ruffle. Gently zigzag your hand while maintaining the same pressure, guiding the piping bag to create the size of ruffle rope you want, then release the pressure and gently lift the piping bag away.

# ASSEMBLING CAKES

Good assembly can make all the difference to the final presentation of your cake. To get a good height on a celebration cake, it's best to bake three or four generous layers in separate tins. You can also bake two deeper cakes and slice each into two layers. These four layers will make an excellent stable foundation for your cake.

## LEVELLING & TORTING

Level a cake by cutting the unwanted dome off the top to make it completely flat. Use the cut-offs to make cake jars and cake pops – you can even freeze them for future use.

Torting is when you slice a cake into two or more even layers. This is useful for making two- or four-layer sponges when you are limited on oven space or equipment and the sponges cannot be baked in separate tins.

You can level and torte a cake using a knife to slice through the sponge, although it can be tricky to achieve precise results this way alone. To guide your knife as you slice through the middle, try the "toothpick" method: At 10 or 12 points around the perimeter of the cake, measure halfway up the sponge with a ruler and push in a toothpick (or cocktail stick) about two-thirds of the way in. Remember to remove all the sticks after you're done!

The most precise method is using a cake leveller. More expensive brands, such as Agbay, are sturdy, accurate and use a blade to slice through sponge easily – a must-have for serious bakers, but certainly not essential for home bakers.

Once stacked, you can check your cake using a spirit level – having perfectly level sponges will help create a stable base for any added tiers and decoration.

## STACKING A CAKE

Smear a small amount of buttercream or ganache onto a cake drum/board and stick the first layer of cake down.

**WITHOUT FILLING:** Spoon the desired amount of buttercream or ganache into the centre of the sponge and spread evenly, almost to the edge, with a palette knife. Alternatively, for a more even layer, pipe a circle of buttercream 1cm (½in) in from the edge of the sponge. Continue to pipe smaller rings inside the circle until completely filled and smooth over with a palette knife. Stack the next layer on top and repeat the process.

**WITH FILLING:** Pipe a buttercream or ganache ring 1cm (½in) in from the perimeter on all but one of your sponges. Chill the sponges in the fridge or freezer for 10–15 minutes or until the rings have solidified – these "dams" will act as a barrier to stop softer fillings spilling out over the edges of your cake. Spoon in your filling of choice. Jam and caramel can be quite sticky, so pop the sponges back in the fridge or freezer for another 10 minutes to set before stacking.

For the top layer of your cake, always turn the final sponge layer over so that the level bottom of the sponge becomes the top of the cake. Place the cake in the fridge for 15–20 minutes to set the buttercream before decorating.

## DOWELLING

While putting support in a tiered cake is imperative, dowelling a one-tier cake is not always necessary. However, if you are baking in warmer weather or plan to place heavy decoration on top of the cake, it will add internal support to prevent the cake from collapsing. We use jumbo plastic bubble straws for dowelling due to their ease of cutting, affordability and strength, but wooden and plastic dowels are also available, if you prefer.

A good rule to remember is to use one dowel per 5cm (2in) of cake, so four dowels for a 20cm (8in) cake, for example. If the cake is tall, we'd suggest adding a few more. Dowel your cake once it is firm and set – dowelling a soft cake may result in the layers sliding or the filling spilling out.

Trim your dowels to the height of the cake and push them down vertically into the centre of the sponge, distributing them evenly in a circular pattern around the perimeter of the cake – but not too close to the edge. The dowels should lay flush to the top of the cake.

If you're not adding heavy decoration to the top, carry on decorating as desired. However, if your cake requires support for heavy decoration, secure a thin cake board on top with some buttercream or ganache and pipe over it to cover the cake board before adding decoration. Always remember to let the recipient of the cake know if it contains dowels!

# CRUMB COATING & APPLYING BUTTERCREAM

Before applying buttercream to a cake, it is often best to crumb coat the cake first. This is the process of covering the outside of the cake with a thin layer of buttercream or ganache to catch excess crumbs before smoothing. It will be partially covered with buttercream, with sponge still showing in places.

## CRUMB COATING

Load some buttercream on a palette knife and pull it around the edges of the chilled cake, adding more buttercream and roughly smoothing it down until the entire side of the cake is covered. Pile some more buttercream on top of the cake and smooth down to the edges using the palette knife.

Working quickly, use a cake scraper to take off any excess buttercream, and smooth what is left around the sponge. The excess buttercream can be reused, however, there may be some crumbs in the mixture.

Smooth down the ragged edge at the top of the cake using a palette knife, before giving the cake a final once over with the cake scraper. Chill the cake until the buttercream has stiffened up. If any ragged edges still remain, trim them off with a small, sharp knife.

**TOP TIP ★** If carefully done, a crumb coat can be used to achieve a semi-naked finish. Our favourite scraper to use is a metal one, which can be heated using hot water to ensure a really smooth finish. If you are using this technique on your cake as the finished result, it is important that you are extremely careful when covering the sponge with buttercream using a palette knife; crumbs are likely to catch in the buttercream and will be visible on the finished cake.

## APPLYING BUTTERCREAM

We like to use a piping bag and cake scraper to achieve a thick, even layer of buttercream over the cake, but you can use a palette knife to spread the buttercream, if you prefer. Make sure your turntable is strong and sturdy or it can shake under the weight of a heavy cake and affect the result.

Crumb coat the cake with buttercream (see left) and chill in the fridge for 10 minutes.

Load buttercream into a piping bag and cut off the end. If the hole is cut too large, the layer of buttercream piped on will be too thick.

Starting at the bottom, pipe even rings of buttercream until the cake is completely covered.

Using a palette knife or scraper, pull the buttercream around the cake and remove the excess until smooth.

You can also use a large, flat piping nozzle (we recommend #789) for a more even application and precision. The buttercream will come out in thin strips, so this technique is ideal if you don't want a thick layer of buttercream on the outside of the cake. It can be difficult to ombre colours or to create a multicoloured technique this way, so we'd use this method for a block colour only.

# SMOOTHING BUTTERCREAM

## USING CAKE SCRAPERS

Cake scrapers are rectangular tools, also known as cake combs, that are used to smooth buttercream or ganache with their straight edges or create elaborate effects with different patterned edges. You can find them made from metal or plastic – both give the same effects but metal ones can be heated under hot water or even a hairdryer (be careful!) to achieve the ultimate smooth finish.

Scrapers are available to buy in many different patterns but depending on the grip of your hand and the pressure applied to the cake, you can even achieve different effects using the same scraper. Patterned scrapers require no more experience than straight-edge scrapers, making them a quick and simple way to give a professional presentation – the technique is the same as the straight-edge scraper.

You can use a straight-edge scraper first to achieve the correct thickness before using the patterned edge. Before using your scraper, check the buttercream is thick enough for the depth of the pattern, as the effect could be compromised if the buttercream is applied too thinly.

Buttercream is more likely to show imperfections if you don't start with the correct consistency, so follow our recipes for perfect buttercream (see page 200) to ensure it isn't too stiff or wet. If you do find the buttercream is a little stiff, just add a few splashes of boiling water from the kettle – we find this smooths buttercream much more successfully than milk or cold water.

Once the buttercream has been piped on, grip the straight-edge scraper with your fingers across the back and with your thumb gripping the front. Fan your fingers out while holding the scraper to apply even pressure.

Hold the scraper at a 45° angle to the cake and smooth the buttercream around the cake. If using a metal scraper, heat it before giving it one final scrape around.

Smooth down the lip of buttercream at the top of the cake with a palette knife before it is chilled, or trim with a sharp knife once chilled.

## THE ULTIMATE SMOOTH FINISH

If you are adding a decoration (chocolate drip, piping, sprinkles or leaf), imperfections can be hidden easily, but if the cake requires complete smoothness, the following tips will help:

**IF BUBBLES APPEAR IN THE BUTTERCREAM:**
Try heating a scraper under a hot tap and giving the cake a once over.

**IF THERE IS A LINE LEFT FROM THE SCRAPER:**
This can be minimized by very gently pulling the scraper from the cake once finished. Some sort of faint line is inevitable, but if there are quite a few lines, there may be a problem with the balance or sturdiness of your turntable.

**IF THE BUTTERCREAM TEARS AWAY FROM THE CAKE:** The texture of the buttercream isn't right. Freeze the cake for 20–30 minutes while making a new batch of buttercream, and then apply a very thin layer on top. The solid layer will help the newly applied buttercream glide on smoothly.

# SCRAPER TECHNIQUES

Using a striped scraper, it is possible to achieve perfect clean stripes quite easily. The trick is to add the first layer of buttercream, then smooth using a striped scraper to create grooves where you will add the other colour, or colours. If you would like a thinner outer layer of buttercream, use less buttercream for the first base coat.

## *STRIPES TECHNIQUE*

Once the buttercream has been applied and smoothed (see pages 209–210), scrape the striped grooves into the cake using a striped scraper. Chill the cake, ideally in the freezer for 20–30 minutes or the fridge for 45–60 minutes, until the buttercream has hardened.

Using a piping bag, fill in the grooves with the colour(s) of your choice. Working quickly against the cold cake, pull the straight edge of the scraper around the cake to scrape off the excess buttercream. The stripes won't yet be visible, but keep scraping and they'll begin to show through. If you work too slowly, the new buttercream stripes may start solidifying against the first colour, which will be more difficult to scrape off.

You may need to apply different pressure to different parts of the cake in order for all the stripes to be clean and neat; if there are marks on the stripes at the top of the cake, for example, apply more pressure at the top of the cake. Apply firm pressure for best results and don't heat the scraper for this part as the colours may blend together if the buttercream starts to melt.

Smooth the buttercream lip at the top of the cake with a palette knife before chilling or trim with a small sharp knife once chilled. Your stripy cake will be ready to decorate after chilling in the fridge for a further 10–15 minutes.

## OMBRE TECHNIQUE

Ombre is not just a trend in hairdressing, it's a popular technique in the cake decorating world, too! Applying colours on the cake in a gradient of shades or blending completely different colours together is quite easy and effective to achieve.

Make your buttercream in the colours and flavours required (see page 200). Apply the buttercream (see page 209) in thick stripes for each colour, working from the top down. There will be an evident split in each colour at this point.

If you want the colours to slightly merge together, run a palette knife around where each section meets to blend and soften the harsh lines. Use a straight-edge scraper to smooth down and scrape off the excess buttercream (see page 210).

Smooth down the buttercream again using a straight-edge or patterned cake scraper (patterned scrapers can be quite forgiving and they help to conceal harsher lines). If using metal equipment, heat the scraper before giving it one final scrape for an extra smooth finish.

Use a palette knife to smooth down the buttercream lip at the top of the cake before it is chilled, or trim with a sharp knife once chilled.

# DRIP TECHNIQUES

The drip effect is a popular choice of decoration and gives the perfect finishing touch to a buttercream cake. There are several different ways you can make a drip for your cake, depending on the desired look, timescale and level of skill required. When adding colour to chocolate, always use an oil-based food colouring as a water or gel-based food colouring will cause the chocolate to seize. These recipes make enough to cover a 20cm (8in) cake.

## CHOCOLATE SPREAD DRIP

100g (½ cup) white chocolate spread
Oil-based food colouring (optional)
Sprinkles/decorations (optional)

The secret ingredient we use on most of our celebration cakes is supermarket own-brand chocolate spread. Some branded chocolate spreads tend to stay thick even when melted, so don't achieve as smooth a drip. If adding colour, start with a white chocolate spread. Most chocolate spreads contain hazelnuts so be sure to check for allergies before using.

Spoon the spread into a microwave-proof bowl or jug. Microwave at full power for 10 seconds at a time until fully melted. Leave the melted spread for a few minutes – until cool but still liquid – this will stop the buttercream on your cake melting and thicken up the spread slightly.

If using food colouring, put one drop at a time into the melted spread and mix, slowly adding more to achieve the desired shade.

With a teaspoon, carefully pool a small amount of the drip mixture on top of the cake, near the edge. Use the spoon to push the spread from the top of the cake over the edge, creating drips in different lengths. The spread will remain tacky rather than drying solid, which is perfect for pushing in individual sprinkles to create an extra special finish. Be careful not to smudge the drips!

## MELTED CHOCOLATE DRIP

100g (3½oz) white chocolate chips, for melting
5ml (1 tsp) vegetable oil
Oil-based food colouring (optional)
Sprinkles/decorations (optional)

Another easy way of creating a drip is by combining melted chocolate with a little vegetable oil. We find this makes the chocolate much smoother, making it perfect to drip down the cake yet still drying relatively hard, which is ideal to use when painting with lustre dust for a metallic drip. This method can be used with white, milk and dark chocolate. If the quality of the chocolate is high, the chocolate drip may not even require any oil.

Melt the chocolate in the microwave at full power for 1 minute and then at 5-second intervals until fully melted. Add the vegetable oil and mix. If you want to colour the drip, add the oil-based food colouring at this point.

Use a teaspoon to carefully pool a small amount of the melted chocolate on the top of the cake, near the edge, and gently push the mixture over the edge to create drips in different lengths.

These chocolate drips will dry hard – the more vegetable oil that is added, the thinner the drips will be and more tacky the chocolate will become, enabling you to add sprinkles and decorations, if desired.

## CHOCOLATE GANACHE DRIP

100g (3½oz) white chocolate chips, for melting

50ml (3½ tbsp) double cream, plus an extra 5–10ml (1–2 tsp)

Oil-based food colouring (optional)

This is probably the most popular way to achieve a drip for a cake. There are differing opinions of how to add the chocolate and the cream, but we find that melting them together creates the best consistency. This technique can be tricky to master as ganache is easy to split – if the mixture is too thick, the drips can look lumpy and if it is too thin, it can run down the cake too easily and become transparent.

Using a 2:1 ratio of white chocolate to double cream, heat together in the microwave at full power for 1 minute at a time until fully melted, then mix. If required, you can also melt over a low heat in a pan on the hob.

Stir the ganache and leave to cool slightly so that it is still liquid but not so hot that it will melt the buttercream on your cake. The ganache should be thick but still thin enough to flow off the spoon. If needed, add an extra 5–10ml (1–2 tsp) of double cream and stir until combined. If using, mix in the oil-based food colouring one drop at a time to achieve your desired colour.

Using a teaspoon, carefully spoon some of the ganache and pool a small amount on top of the cake, near the edge. With the spoon, gently nudge the mixture from the top of the cake over the edge to create drips of different lengths.

The state of ganache once dry will depend on the amount of cream that was added – the more white chocolate that the ganache contains, the harder the drip will dry.

## CARAMEL DRIP

A caramel drip is perfect for sticky toffee pudding and other caramel-themed cakes. Caramel can be bought in jars ready to use but if you want to make it from scratch, follow the recipe on page 21 and allow it to cool before using. Melt in a couple of squares of white chocolate while heating the caramel to help the drip firm up and stay in place all day. Caramel drips will never set hard, however, you should be able to add light sprinkles without affecting the shape of the drip.

## UPSIDE-DOWN DRIP

The upside-down drip is an effective way to add a drip to a cake with a difference - gravity defying! The process is a simple one: create drips using your chosen method and allow them to set, then flip the cake upside down! We recommend sandwiching the cake between two cake boards to turn it over fairly easily.

### TOP TIPS

★ These mixtures can also be loaded into a squeezy bottle to apply with more accuracy, if preferred.

★ Add sprinkles to the drips by using tweezers or wetting your finger and pressing it into some sprinkles, then carefully onto the individual drips.

★ Make sure the drips are dry before decorating the top of the cake - we recommend putting it back in the fridge to chill for 30 minutes.

# TEMPERING CHOCOLATE

There are various specialist techniques that chocolatiers use to temper chocolate, however, we've got some tricks up our sleeves for you, so that anyone can do it.

Every chocolate bar that you buy is already tempered, which is great if you want to eat it – it snaps in your mouth, tastes smooth and won't start melting too quickly when handled. When melted beyond certain temperatures, chocolate loses its temper as the crystals in the cocoa butter begin to misbehave. If left to re-solidify, untempered chocolate will never fully set and will be dull and waxy rather than shiny.

Chocolate with a high percentage of cocoa butter (over 31 per cent for dark chocolate and over 25 per cent for milk chocolate and white chocolate) will give better results and it's better to use more chocolate than needed, as it is easier to control the temperature of higher volumes of chocolate. Surplus chocolate can be spread over a baking sheet and broken up once set to reuse at a later date. If tempering less than 100g (3½oz) of chocolate, halve the times listed here.

## MICROWAVE METHOD

This easy method melts already-tempered chocolate so gently that it doesn't come out of its tempered state, and so doesn't need to be re-tempered.

Break the chocolate into small pieces, or use callets (chocolate chips for melting). Put the chocolate into a plastic, microwave-proof bowl (ceramic bowls can heat up quickly, which means it will be more likely for your chocolate to overheat).

Blast the chocolate in the microwave at full power for 1 minute and then stir. The chocolate may not look like it has changed at this stage, but stirring will help distribute the heat throughout the chocolate.

Blast the chocolate for a further 30 seconds. Stir again. The chocolate should start to melt.

Microwave the chocolate at full power for 5–10 seconds at a time (it can be a slow process), stirring each time until there are still just a few lumps left in the chocolate. This is where you should stop heating the chocolate, as the lumps will melt on their own if you continue to stir. If they do not look like they will melt, blast again for another 5 seconds.

> **TOP TIP** ★ You can melt tempered chocolate using a bain-marie (a heatproof bowl set over a pan of hot water on the hob), but it is harder to keep the temperature under control. Instead, take the pan off the heat while the chocolate melts slowly over it. You can put it back on the heat if the melting slows down.

## SEEDING METHOD

This requires melting the chocolate with less precision and re-tempering it by adding in solid already-tempered chocolate at the end. You will need a sugar thermometer for this method.

Break up the chocolate into small pieces, or use callets. Set one-third of the chocolate to the side.

Add 2.5cm (1in) of water to the saucepan and simmer over a low heat. Place a heatproof bowl over the saucepan, making sure no steam can escape. Add two-thirds of the chocolate into the bowl.

Stir the chocolate until completely melted and keep checking the temperature of the chocolate using your thermometer. The chocolate must not reach any higher than the following temperatures:
*White chocolate: 43°C (109°F)*
*Milk chocolate: 46°C (115°F)*
*Dark chocolate: 48°C (118°F)*

Take the bowl off the heat and add in the remaining one-third of the chocolate. The solid chocolate will melt under the heat of the already-melted chocolate, dispersing stable cocoa butter crystals back into the mixture. Keep checking the temperature of your chocolate – it should cool to the following temperatures:
*White chocolate: 26°C (79°F)*
*Milk chocolate: 27°C (81°F)*
*Dark chocolate: 28°C (82°F)*

If you need to improve the fluidity of the chocolate, place the bowl back over the saucepan of warm water to reheat a little (the residual heat will likely be enough to gently warm the chocolate through). The chocolate should reach the following temperatures:
*White chocolate: 28°C (82°F)*
*Milk chocolate: 30°C (86°F)*
*Dark chocolate: 32°C (90°F)*

**TOP TIP** ★ To test your chocolate, smear a little on a palette knife or a sheet of greaseproof paper. Tempered chocolate should dry quickly, within 4–6 minutes, and will snap nicely when dried.

# TERMS & TRANSLATIONS

| British ingredients | American ingredients |
| --- | --- |
| bicarbonate of soda | baking soda |
| Biscoff biscuits | Belgian wafer cookies |
| Biscoff spread | creamy cookie butter, Trader Joe's Speculoos Butter is an ideal substitute |
| biscuits | cookies |
| black treacle | molasses |
| candy floss | cotton candy |
| caster sugar | superfine sugar |
| chocolate spread | Trader Joe's has a chocolate/almond spread, US bakers can find Cadbury chocolate spread online at Amazon |
| cornflour | cornstarch |
| digestive biscuits | Graham crackers |
| double cream | heavy cream |
| flaked almonds | sliced almonds |
| ginger biscuits | ginger thins cookies, such as Anna's or Peek Freans Ginger Crisps |
| golden syrup | Light corn syrup is a barely adequate substitute. Whole Foods usually stocks authentic golden syrup. |
| icing sugar | confectioners' sugar |
| Jammie Dodgers | jelly ring cookies |
| Lotus biscuits | see Biscoff biscuits |
| Lotus spread | see Biscoff spread |
| mixed spice | apple pie spice |
| plain flour | all-purpose flour |
| self-raising flour | self-rising flour |
| soured cream | sour cream |
| sponge | cake |
| sultanas | golden raisins |

| British equipment | American equipment |
| --- | --- |
| cake drum | cake board |
| cake scraper | cake icing smoother or comb (available at Wilton's) |
| cake tin | cake pan |
| cling film | plastic wrap |
| cocktail stick | toothpick |
| hob | stovetop burner |
| nozzle | piping tip |
| piping bag | pastry bag |
| sugar thermometer | candy thermometer |

# CONVERSIONS

If required, we recommend you follow the conversions as listed on the individual recipes, however, here is a handy list of standard conversions should you need them for anything else.

**Dry measures**

| | |
|---|---|
| 15g | ½oz |
| 30g | 1oz |
| 60g | 2oz |
| 90g | 3oz |
| 125g | 4oz (¼lb) |
| 155g | 5oz |
| 185g | 6oz |
| 220g | 7oz |
| 250g | 8oz (½lb) |
| 280g | 9oz |
| 315g | 10oz |
| 345g | 11oz |
| 375g | 12oz (¾lb) |
| 410g | 13oz |
| 440g | 14oz |
| 470g | 15oz |
| 500g | 16oz (1lb) |
| 750g | 24oz (1½lb) |
| 1kg | 32oz (2lb) |

**Volume measures**

| | |
|---|---|
| 75ml | 2½fl oz |
| 90ml | 3fl oz |
| 100ml | 3½fl oz |
| 120ml | 4fl oz |
| 150ml | 5fl oz |
| 200ml | 7fl oz |
| 240ml | 8fl oz |
| 250ml | 9fl oz |
| 300ml | 10fl oz |
| 350ml | 12fl oz |
| 400ml | 14fl oz |
| 450ml | 15fl oz |
| 500ml | 16fl oz |
| 600ml | 1 pint |
| 750ml | 1¼ pints |
| 900ml | 1½ pints |
| 1 litre | 1¾ pints |
| 1.2 litres | 2 pints |
| 1.4 litres | 2½ pints |
| 1.5 litres | 2¾ pints |
| 1.7 litres | 3 pints |
| 2 litres | 3½ pints |
| 3 litres | 5¼ pints |

**Length measures**

| | |
|---|---|
| 3mm | ⅛in |
| 6mm | ¼in |
| 1cm | ½in |
| 2cm | ¾in |
| 2.5cm | 1in |
| 5cm | 2in |
| 6cm | 2½in |
| 8cm | 3in |
| 10cm | 4in |
| 13cm | 5in |
| 15cm | 6in |
| 18cm | 7in |
| 20cm | 8in |
| 22cm | 9in |
| 25cm | 10in |
| 28cm | 11in |
| 30cm | 12in (1ft) |

**Oven temperatures**

| | |
|---|---|
| 130°C | 110°C fan/250°F/Gas ½ |
| 140°C | 120°C fan/275°F/Gas 1 |
| 150°C | 130°C fan/300°F/Gas 2 |
| 160°C | 140°C fan/325°F/Gas 3 |
| 180°C | 160°C fan/350°F/Gas 4 |
| 190°C | 170°C fan/375°F/Gas 5 |
| 200°C | 180°C fan/400°F/Gas 6 |
| 220°C | 200°C fan/425°F/Gas 7 |
| 230°C | 210°C fan/455°F/Gas 8 |
| 240°C | 220°C fan/475°F/Gas 9 |

**Australian tablespoon conversions to UK spoon measures**

| | |
|---|---|
| ½ tbsp | 2 tsp |
| 1 tbsp | 1 heaped tbsp |
| 2 tbsp (8 tsp) | 2½ tbsp |
| 3 tbsp (12 tsp) | 4 tbsp |
| 4 tbsp (16 tsp) | 5 tbsp |
| 5 tbsp (20 tsp) | 6½ tbsp |
| 6 tbsp (24 tsp) | 8 tbsp |

# INDEX

**Project Editor** Lucy Sienkowska
**Senior Designer** Tania Gomes
**Jacket Coordinator** Jasmin Lennie
**DTP Designers** Satish Gaur, Umesh Singh Rawat
**DTP Coordinator** Tarun Sharma
**Pre-Production Manager** Balwant Singh
**Production Editor** David Almond
**Senior Production Controller** Stephanie McConnell
**Editorial Director** Cara Armstrong
**Publishing Director** Katie Cowan
**Art Director** Maxine Pedliham

**Copy Editor** Vicky Orchard
**Designer** Jack Watkins
**Photography** Jessica Griffiths
**Food Stylist** Dominique Eloïse Alexander
**Prop Stylist** Faye Wears
**Proofreader** Anne Sheasby
**Indexer** Vanessa Bird

First published in Great Britain in 2023 by
Dorling Kindersley Limited
DK, One Embassy Gardens, 8 Viaduct Gardens,
London, SW11 7BW

The authorised representative in the EEA is
Dorling Kindersley Verlag GmbH.
Arnulfstr. 124, 80636 Munich, Germany

**For the curious**
www.dk.com

## Authors' Acknowledgments

Thank you to Cara, Lucy, Vicky, Tania and everyone at DK for asking us back, being patient with us and helping our vision come alive. To Dom and Jess who have worked with us to create the most beautifully photographed book (again!), you're both amazing at your jobs.

Thank you to the baking community who continue to support one another, repost and share tips, recipes, designs and work that genuinely inspires people – from professionals to hobby bakers.

Thank you to our parents, families, husbands, children, friends and everyone who has helped us with our business somewhere along the way. Thank you to our customers and followers for continuing to support us, buy from us and love our products. Thank you to our colleagues past and present, who help us run the business day-to-day and keep us going, through good times and bad! We would be nowhere without you.

Thank you to anyone who invests time in us or in our business – we never dreamt we would be here 10 years ago when we first started. It's an incredible journey we're loving being on together. Thanks,

*Lauren & Rachel x*

To see all the treats, equipment and baking ingredients that Finch Bakery has to offer, visit **www.finchbakery.com**